Before Television

Before Television

The Radio Years

Glenhall Taylor

South Brunswick and New York: A. S. Barnes and Company
London: Thomas Yoseloff Ltd

A. S. Barnes and Co., Inc.
Cranbury, New Jersey 08512

Thomas Yoseloff Ltd
Magdalen House
136–148 Tooley Street
London SE1 2TT, England

Library of Congress Cataloging in Publication Data

Taylor, Glenhall, 1903-
    Before television.

    Includes index.
    1.   Radio programs--United States.   I.   Title.
PN1991.3.U6T39   791.44'0973   78-69644
ISBN 0-498-02204-8

PRINTED IN THE UNITED STATES OF AMERICA

for
Barbara
The critic on my hearth

Contents

Acknowledgments

I would like the following people to know how much I appreciate the help they extended to me during the gestation period of the brainchild tucked between these two covers. Their help was especially valuable in three areas: supplying information which I lacked, jogging my memory on people, dates and places and, of course, in lending me many of the photographs which have been used to illustrate this book. To borrow a line from Irving Berlin's famous song, "There's no people like show people." Among them are:

The Academy of Motion Picture Arts and Sciences, George Balzer, Ted Bliss, True Boardman, Phil Cohan, Norman Corwin, Ken Darby, Jerry Devine, Michael B. Druxman, Family Theater, Inc., Dolores Finlay, Paul Franklin, Kenneth Greenwald, David C. Hall, Martin Halperin, Jerry Hausner, Don Hills, William R. Howard III, Dan Jenkins, Jim and Gretchen Jordan, Dorothy Lamour, Muzzy Marcellino, Frank O'Connor, Austin Peterson, Pacific Pioneer Broadcasters, Charles Price, Jewel Smith, Harfield Weedin, Paul Weirick, Paula Winslowe, Ron Wolf, and Earl Zeigler.

Before Television

1

Tuning in

at the Beginning

In the year 1887, German physicist Heinrich Hertz wired an electric charge to a condenser, short-circuited it through a spark gap and produced electromagnetic waves. In 1892, American inventor Nathan B. Stubblefield became the first person to transmit a voice without the use of wires; it was heard a mile away from the transmitter.* By 1901, an Italian electrical engineer, Guglielmo Marconi, sent a wireless telegraphy message across the Atlantic. In 1907, another American inventor, Lee De Forest, patented a tube—the "triode". From then on science progressed so rapidly that by 1922, an advertiser could buy a ten-minute time segment on WEAF, New York City, for $100. What wonders lay ahead!

There was the excitement of tinkering with the "cat's whisker" on a crystal receiver and listening, via earphones, to unamplified music and speech. Later, there was the thrill of hearing the amplified, effulgent sounds of the New York Philharmonic, Edward R. Murrow's graphic, on-the-spot reporting of the bombing of London during World War II, the clattering avalanche of junk spilling from Fibber McGee's unkempt closet, and phonograph records. Still later would come "radio with pictures" and television screens would light up living rooms with the Boston

---

* *Kentucky Progress Magazine,* vol. 2, no. 7.

Jim Jordan and his wife, Marian, as they appeared at the height of their popularity as "Fibber McGee and Molly" in their weekly radio series.

"Pops" Orchestra, live camera reporting of the Vietnamese conflict, comedian Red Skelton's pratfalls, and old movies.

The author of this rambling reminiscence is fortunate to have lived through much of the history created by early radio and television. On May 11, 1922, I made my radio debut on the old "Rockridge" station, KZY, in Berkeley, California, as one-third of a trio—violin, banjo and piano. I was the pianist. The studio, in a large home in the Berkeley hills, was furnished in wicker, suggesting it had once been a sun room. But now, incongruously, there were a grand piano and bench, control panels, and a miscellany of other electronic gear. The microphones, to my then-inexperienced eye, appeared to be merely old-fashioned telephone transmitters, their black, hard-rubber mouthpieces protruding from the sides of cube-shaped wooden boxes. One box was placed in front of the violinist, another before the banjoist, and the third rested on the sounding board beneath the raised lid of the piano. To us, as a first experience for our trio, the program seemed remarkable. However, from the listeners' standpoint, the important feature of the program was prominent educator David Starr Jordan, Stanford University's first President Emeritus. His radio-debut address drew favorable comment from the press; our inspired performance drew no comment whatsoever.

In May, 1927, the National Broadcasting Company (NBC) created the "Orange" Network of 7 Western-States stations* for the purpose of celebrating the "Yale Round-the-World Dinner" —an endowment-fund-raising event with hundreds of Yale alumni attending banquets in every important city in the United States; all held at the same hour in each time zone. Since there was no permanent coast to coast hookup at that time, several eastern stations joined in beaming a separate program to cities on the Atlantic side of the nation. Provost Henry S. Graves of the class of 1892, a former chief of the United States Forestry Service, spoke over the Orange Network. The list of speakers participating in the eastern broadcast was headed by Chief Justice William Howard Taft.

Gerard Chatfield, then National Program Director for the

---

* KFI, Los Angeles; KPO, San Francisco; KGO, Oakland; KGW, Portland; KOMO and KFOA, Seattle; KHQ, Spokane.

Glenhall Taylor & His Radio Music Makers as they appeared just before performing on NBC's first Pacific Coast network hookup in 1926. (The author is seated with the accordion on his lap).

network, engaged my dance orchestra for the event. The NBC staff quartet, "The Olympians", masquerading as collegians, and two extra banjos augmented my regular ten piece band to give a "Joe College" touch. Thus occurred my first *network* experience. In the five short years after I played my first radio engagement the broadcasting business had progressed rapidly despite my minor artistic contributions.

Parenthetically, although thirty-eight radio stations had participated in a coast-to-coast broadcast of the Radio Industries Banquet in New York City on the 17th of September, 1926, and additional broadcasts were subsequently released across the nation, the first *regularly* scheduled transcontinental broadcasts were inaugurated on November 26th of that year. The following excerpt, announcing the event, is from a *San Francisco Examiner* news item on Wednesday, the 24th:

Radio's famous "Amos 'n' Andy": Freeman Gosden (l.) and Charles Correll—Amos 'n' Andy respectively—at the microphone with singer/ actress Marilyn Maxwell.

Announcer Bill Hay celebrated his 90th birthday in 1977 and was saluted by members of the Pacific Pioneers Broadcasters. Bill's voice was heard by millions as, five times a week, he happily intoned, "Ladies and gentlemen . . . Amos 'n' Andy!"

The Radio Corporation of America, which has heretofore confined its broadcasting activities to the Eastern stations, announces that it will present regular Friday evening programs over KGO, commencing this week. The hour assigned is from 8 to 9 o'clock. KGO has been silent on Friday nights.

The once-a-week scheduling of transcontinental broadcasts would remain standard operating procedure for many weeks to come, but early in 1927 daily scheduling would become effective. By August of that year "Amos 'n' Andy" would keep the nation's ears glued to their sets for ten minutes, Mondays through Fridays.

But this is not a history of broadcasting. Rather, it is a collage of anecdotes and the reminiscences of one of the industry's pioneers. Or, to use a younger generation's epithet often applied to the likes of me, "one of the *old* farts." That onomatopoeic word, incidentally, brings to mind an occasion upon which it

Grover Jones (l.), screen writer who devised many of the plots for "Silver Theater" programs, is seen in a script conference with actor James Stewart.

was used with delightful accuracy to describe one of early radio's oft recurring dilemmas:

In the late 1930's I was employed to produce a CBS network series called "Silver Theater," an "anthology" of half hour dramas. To lend a fresh slant to the dramatic material, we had hired an eminent screen writer, Grover Jones, to supply original story outlines. Because Grover was unfamiliar with radio-script format, our regular staff writer supplied the adaptations. After a few weeks of our three-way collaboration at his home, Grover, who had never been in a radio studio, expressed a desire to attend a "dress" rehearsal and broadcast.

During the rehearsal he sat with us in the control room, utterly fascinated with what he watched through the huge double-paned window. On the stage of the large audience studio in Hollywood's Columbia Square, the sound-effects men, orchestra, actors and actresses were being coordinated into a single, well-oiled unit, guided by directions given over the talk-back in the control room. When the control room clock's second hand arrived "straight up" on the hour, an "On the Air" sign lit up in the studio and everyone onstage was like a horse at the starting gate. Our screenwriter friend marveled that from the moment my hand came down with a forefinger pointed at the orchestra conductor, fate was my copilot. (The reader should bear in mind this was before the advent of magnetic tape recording.)

Accustomed to seeing film directors order another "take" if a scene didn't play just right and knowing that film techniques permitted sound-track corrections (or remedying imperfect sound-effect and orchestral balances), he was actually aghast that once the "live" broadcast commenced, there were no opportunities to correct mistakes. He summed up the situation better than we had ever heard it summed up before:

"My God!" he exclaimed. "If anyone makes a mistake, it's like a fart at a party! You can't take it back."

There were, of course, plenty of mistakes. Many of them have been repeated until they've become cliches. Many have been told so often that errors have crept in to the extent that the origin of the "blooper" sometimes becomes vague, or the name of the person committing it forever lost in limbo. I have heard one little beauty accredited to so many different kiddie program hosts that, by now, I sadly admit it may even be apocryphal. I first heard the anecdote in San Francisco in the late twenties with the perpetrator identified as Jack Keogh of radio station KPO. After signing off his storyteller's program with a saccharine "good bye" to the kiddies, Jack, (so the story went) thinking his microphone had been safely switched off, turned to the studio engineer and said, "There . . . I guess that'll hold the little bastards for a while."

But I have since heard it told about "Uncle John" Daggett of KHJ, Los Angeles, and "Uncle Don" in New York. Other bloopers, such as Harry Von Zell's birthday greeting to the President of the United States, "Congratulations, Hoobert Heever!," have been authenticated by the perpetrators themselves. Some, of course, I have personally "earwitnessed":

Many years ago, on the Al Pearce Show, I had carefully rehearsed a substitute announcer in a commercial for Grape

Nuts (long before Euell Gibbons discovered the cereal reminded him of wild hickory nuts) until he had it down pat. But on the air, coast-to-coast, he belted out loud and clear: "Be sure to buy grapefruit!"

And I nearly fell out of my chair when, listening to the radio, I heard an announcer recommend, "Give your wife a gorgeous Gruen for Christmas." Of course, that's not so bad in print (as the copywriter undoubtedly discovered later), but when read aloud with the word "gorgeous" eliding into "Gruen," it comes out as a very nice Christmas present, indeed—something to be enjoyed by *both* husband and wife.

From 1928 until 1943, NBC operated two networks—the "Blue," which in the latter year became the American Broadcasting Company (ABC), and the "Red," the more commercial of the two. In NBC's San Francisco studios, the announcers' booth contained a panel of switches and signal lights known to its users as the "announcers' delight." Upon hearing the network cue, the announcer on duty would flip the proper switch to open the mike for the local station's call-letter identification, an act which required a certain degree of concentration. On this particular morning in 1931, KPO—feeding the Red network—was carrying its daily "happy time" program, "The Shell Ship of Joy" (sponsored by the Shell Oil Company), with its "skipper", Hugh Barrett Dobbs, as the master of ceremonies. Simultaneously, KGO—hooked into the Blue Network—was transmitting the first world-wide broadcast of Pope Pius XI who was making a plea in behalf of global peace. A friend of mine, veteran announcer Cecil Underwood, was on duty when the network cue for the "happy time" program was given: "This is the Red Network of the National Broadcasting Company."

Cecil snapped to, and flipped the switch. Unaware he had opened the mike for KGO on the *Blue* Network, he cut into the Pope's address with, "The past hour of fun and nonsense has come to you over KPO, San Francisco." He told me later that the network's telephone switchboard lit up like a pinball machine with complaint calls and that NBC ultimately made a formal apology to the area archdiocese.

A similar impiety—though local, not on a network—occurred on KTAB (now KSFO), the Pickwick Broadcasting Corporation's

San Francisco-Oakland station which I then managed. It was on a Sunday morning and the Reverend Phillips of Oakland's Tenth Avenue Baptist Church was fervently preaching a sermon from his pulpit as the station carried the broadcast by remote control. Standing by in the KTAB Oakland studio was an announcer, engrossed in the comic section of the Sunday paper. It was the custom, whenever a remote control broadcast was in progress, to have a phonograph record on the turntable ready to fill in dead air in the event of a line failure. The announcer, of course, had no reason to anticipate such an emergency, for the Sunday-sermon broadcasts had been a regular feature for years without mishap. Except on that day:

The line suddenly went dead, and a second or two elapsed before the announcer realized what had happened. He then acted quickly and efficiently: he dropped his paper, switched on the turntable and spun the record. Raucous jazz music blared forth with Cab Calloway himself singing in his gravel-voiced tones, "You'll Never Get to Heaven That Way." Peace on earth was eventually restored, but it took some fast explaining.

Al Ryan was a good announcer but occasionally had trouble with foreign words. I was sitting at my program director's desk at KTAB one day when he entered my office to ask how to pronounce *hors d'oeuvres* in a spot announcement for a local delicatessen. I gave him the Anglicized version "ore derve," which he repeated several times until I assured him he had it correct. As he hurried back into the studio, I switched on my loudspeaker and listened. Following a musical selection, his clear, mellow voice came through with his usual authority, the words of the commercial nicely articulated until he came to the final line:

"In addition to these specialties, the Blank Delicatessen carries a complete line of whore's doors."

At this late date, I don't recall whether there were any repercussions. In retrospect, however, it's possible the sponsor may have had a good response from male members of the audience.

More than one announcer had difficulty with a word combination in the Greyhound Bus Lines commercial which described the beauties of the New Mexico scenery which might be observed from the bus windows. Whenever we heard a new announcer tackle the commercial, we awaited the stumbling block with macabre enjoyment. The copy referred to the Indians' "crumbling, quaint cliff dwellings", and the chances were about 50–50 it would come out a spoonerism: "crumbling, claint *quiff* dwellings". (It's possible there was some quiff dwelling going on behind those whore's doors).

Other "smutterings," innocently spoken, often burst from loudspeakers to shock thousands of listeners. One such boo-boo came from the announcers' booth at San Francisco's famed Mark Hopkins Hotel from whence, in the late 1920's, station KFRC regularly broadcast, by remote control, dance music from the elegant dining room, Peacock Court. One evening, cutting into the broadcast to give a station identification, the announcer poked the button on his control panel and proclaimed, "The music of Eddie Harkness and his Orchestra is coming to you from Pea-court Cock."

He immediately attempted a correction but the spoonerism persisted as he said, "I mean, Peacourt *Cock*."

Aghast, he pressed the button to isolate himself from his public, took a deep breath, poked the button again and said, authoritatively, ". . . Peacourt *Cock*!" He then cut off the mike once more and slumped helplessly in his chair.

But my deepest sympathy went out to KTAB sports announcer Ernie Smith, who during baseball season was forced to exercise constant, tension-building vigilance while excitedly calling plays in which one of the San Francisco Seals' star players participated. Imagine, having to say in a hurry, "Mike Hunt is heading for home!"

~~~~~~~~~~~~~~~~~~~~~~~~~

While much of KTAB's programming was "live," some of it consisted of phonograph records, especially in the early morning and late evening. The station's transmitter was in Oakland, across the bay from San Francisco, but the main studio and business offices were in the Pickwick Hotel in the latter city. This meant that the announcer might be on duty by himself—particularly in the morning before the business offices opened up—reading commercials and spinning his own phonograph records. With no recorded commercials in those days, and the average recording of a popular song seldom running over three minutes, it was sometimes difficult to find time in which to answer Mother Nature's call. And most people are certainly aware of how urgent those calls may be after a cup or two of hot morning coffee.

To one of San Francisco's early-day popular announcers, the now long-departed James Kendrick, goes the credit for solving this problem—at least temporarily. In the station's record library was a then rare item: an electrical transcription. These transcriptions, nowadays seldom seen, were huge disks 16 inches in diameter, played at the then unusual speed of 33⅓ revolutions per minute. The running time was approximately fifteen minutes. Jimmy, often alone on duty in the early morning, found it very convenient to play this récording during a session in the men's room. For the enlightenment of his fellow announcers, he scrawled across the label, in bold, black letters, two words:

CRAPPING RECORD

On one particular morning, Jimmy started the record and headed confidently for the bathroom. What he was unaware of was that through wear and tear, the record had developed a flawed groove. Thus it was that with the studio sounds shut out by a closed door, he was happily oblivious to what was going out over the air: the primitive voices of a country-western group were bleating out the famous ballad "Home on the Range" when the needle stuck in the damaged groove. What the radio audience heard was something like, "Oh, give me a home/ Where the buffalo clunk/ buffalo clunk, buffalo clunk, buffalo clunk . . . "

Fortunately, I arrived at the studio in time to prevent the buffalo from clunking all over the studio. Hearing the malfunctioning "corral" group, I raced into the control room, lifted the tone arm, and substituted a "pop" record on one of the 78-RPM turntables. Just as I went looking for Jimmy, the men's room door opened and he emerged.

"Oh, boy—I sure feel better!" he said with a smile and a sigh of relief, unaware of what had been happening.

"Your crapping record was stuck," I informed him sternly.

"So was I," he grinned. Then, realizing the import of what I'd just told him, his jaw dropped. Recovering, he added, "I'm glad I didn't know about the record. It's terrible to get caught like that with your pants down."

We got caught with our switchboard down, too: the unattended PBX, swamped with calls from listeners, buzzed like a hornets' nest until the operator came on duty at 9:00 o'clock and pulled the jack cords.

~~~~~~~~~~~~~~~~~~~~~~~~~~~~~~

KTAB's big feature program of the week was a two hour show called "Pepper Box Revue." It featured the station's staff artists—vocalists, instrumentalists, comedians—and a feature spot or two by the orchestra which I conducted. The master of ceremonies was the station manager, Bob Roberts. Bob had a good sense of humor and liked his introductions to the various artists and sketches laced with comedy. He especially enjoyed garbled or phony song titles, no matter how corny. The writers obliged by supplying him with such brash bits of maize as "Ireland Can't be Heaven, My Wife's Mother Came from There," "She Was a Spanish Fisherman's Daughter, and How She Could Cast-a-net," or "Run into the Roundhouse, Nellie, He Can't Corner You in There."

On one program, in a spot where Bob would introduce an orchestra selection, the script gave him an *ersatz* title with which he was particularly delighted. Radio was quite conservative in the late twenties and early thirties; there were many "no-nos" governing not only what slang words one might use, but a strict taboo on the use of certain words such as "diaper", "nuts" (unless in a cooking recipe), "fanny", "pratfall", "virgin" (unless in a Biblical sense), "cock" (even when it referred to a rooster), and "manure" unless it had to do with garden fertilizing). We decided to be daring and use the latter "no-no" word by implication. Bob would introduce the orchestra number thus:

"And now the Pepper Box Revue Orchestra will be heard in the popular tune, 'She Was Only a Stableman's Daughter, but All the Horsemen Were Acquainted with Her'."

At the proper moment, Bob stepped to the microphone. I raised my hand, ready to give the orchestra the downbeat. My hand reminded aloft for what seemed minutes, for Bob, drawing one of those inexplicable blanks, was carried forward in the speech by his own momentum:

"And now," he began, "the Pepper Box Revue Orchestra will be heard in the popular tune, 'She Was Only a Stableman's Daughter, but All the . . .' He panicked for an instant, then plunged ahead, articulating ever so carefully lest he offend: '. . . Horsemen . . . *Knew* . . . *Her*'."

After a horrible moment of suspense, I brought down my hand. The orchestra's "attack" on the opening measures could hardly be called that. Instead of launching into the selection cleanly and precisely as it had been rehearsed, the hilariously laughing musicians sputtered into their trumpets and trombones, pooped into their saxophones, and squeaked their fiddles. Only the drummer was precise. But his foot came down so hard on the pedal of his bass drum he nearly knocked us off the air.

Bob commented after the program, "I thought for a minute I'd *stepped* in some."

"I thought you had, too," said one of the musicians, handing him a broom.

Luckily, there were no complaints from listeners.

In the depression years following the October, 1929, stock market crash, numerous business firms slashed their advertising expenditures and radio felt the pinch along with other industries and individuals. Because sales personnel had been reduced, many stations—KTAB among them—welcomed additional revenue from time brokers. The time broker was usually an aggressive man-on-the-run, often carrying his "office" around in a brief case. Because his expenses were minimal, he could afford to put in most of his time calling on small businesses or large companies with small budgets for certain individual products, selling spot announcements at less than it would cost a radio station to send out a salesman to *try* to make a sale. When the time broker had enough contracts in his pocket, he'd contact a radio station with a proposition to purchase quarter, half, or even full hour time segments "across the board"—usually Mondays through

Fridays. Eager for additional income, many stations, including KTAB, would create a "wholesale" rate at a price the broker could afford. He, in turn, would supply his own announcer and programs—sometimes phonograph records, sometimes "live" talent.

An aggressive time broker would load his time segments with commercials, sometimes jamming in twelve to fifteen one-minute spots in a half hour. One such broker was a bright and happy little dynamo named Jack Hall. Jack had a thirty minute time slot Mondays through Fridays on KTAB. He did his own announcing, and his talent was a nimble-fingered pianist by the name of Clem Kennedy.

Among Jack's sponsors was a wine-grape grower located some fifty miles north of San Francisco in Napa County. Naturally, prohibition had imposed certain restrictions on the wine business, and the vineyardist, trying for an "honest buck" as the saying went in those days, turned to selling grapevine cuttings by mail. He advertised his mail order business on Jack's programs. Jack really put his heart into it while reading the commercials for this sponsor. I was soon to learn why:

One day he came to me and asked. "How'd you like to do me a favor and announce my program one afternoon this week?"

Jack explained that he had to pay a call on the vineyardist and, because the trip and the contract renewal negotiations would kill the better part of a day, he was afraid he might not be able to make the round trip from San Francisco and back in time to handle the program himself. Because he was a valued client, I agreed to help.

When the day came, I placed Jack's loose-leaf binder with its typewritten commercial copy on a music stand and adjusted it into position before the microphone, signaled Clem Kennedy who sat at the piano in the same studio, and the program began. During the first half of the program, I did what I modestly considered to be an excellent job of substituting for Jack, until I came to a spot announcement for Ex-Lax, a proprietary medicine for the relief of constipation.

It was Jack's custom, whenever pressed for time during his half-hour programs, to have the studio engineer lower the volume of the piano mike while he announced over the background music. Glancing at the clock as I began the Ex-Lax commercial, I decided we'd better save a minute or so, and signaled the engineer to fade the piano. I was well into the commercial when, over the top of the music stand, I glimpsed Clem grinning at me over his shoulder, his fingers still dancing along the keyboard. In the control room, the engineer was shaking with laughter. For a moment I wondered what in hell they thought was so funny. Seeing my puzzled expression, Clem played louder. Then it dawned on me: he was accompanying my Ex-Lax "fight constipation" pitch with a happy, up-tempo rendition of the then popular song, "Runnin' Wild!" I, too, ran wild. Sputtering in an attempt to control my laughter and swallowing every other syllable, I barely made it to the end of the commercial. I was afraid Jack might have lost the *Ex-Lax* account because of my lousing up the spot announcement; however, on his return, Jack laughed like hell. I was somewhat petulant (wounded professional pride, I suppose) when I asked him, "Why did you have to drive a hundred miles to renew the deal? Couldn't you have sent the contract to Old Joe Vineyard and had him send your payment by mail?"

Jack grinned. "He can't send his payments by mail. He doesn't pay by check. He pays by the jug."

It was then I learned that this was one of Jack's "swap deals". Each time the vineyardist's contract came up for renewal, Jack would drive up to Napa County and return with an assortment of gallon jugs containing port, sherry, "Dago red", and—especially appreciated during Prohibition days— grappa, that potent, unaged brandy distilled from grape pomace.

Jack presented me with a jug as a reward for services over and beyond the call of duty. It was good grappa, and it nicely salved my wounded pride.

~~~~~~~~~~~~~~~~~~~~~~~~

I was with the Pickwick Broadcasting Corporation for four and a half years, a year and a quarter of which I spent as manager of the company's station, KTM, in Los Angeles. When I was assigned to that position, my boss, Henry Hohman, warned me that none of the station's employees nor any of its sponsors should know that I'd played piano professionally or that I had engaged in other entertainment activities on the sister station in San Francisco. I was to be 100 percent businessman.

I played my new role to the hilt and probably would have kept it up indefinitely, but Henry was a piano buff. KTM had an informal Saturday night variety program, and it was Hank's habit to sit in the station lobby with the other spectators, watching the performances through the big glass window of the studio. One night he beckoned me to his side and said, "Get in there and play something."

I reminded him of his warning against appearing in a role other than that of a businesslike station manager. "Aw, what the hell," he said, "none of our clients will know if your name isn't mentioned."

With that, he instructed the master of ceremonies to announce me as a "guest artist who wishes to remain anonymous." Then he ordered me to "Play 'Twelfth Street Rag' the way you used to in San Francisco." And so I played. After all, he'd convinced me that nobody in the radio audience would know it was I, so our secret would not be violated.

I had no sooner returned to the lobby when the switchboard operator informed me there was a call waiting for me. I picked up the phone. A voice asked, "Hey—are you Glenhall Taylor?"

I confessed. Excitedly, the voice continued: "Glen, this is Frankie, from San Francisco!"

Puzzled, I asked, "Frankie who?"

"Frankie, the bootlegger! I thought that was you the minute I heard 'Twelfth Street Rag.' I'd recognize your playing that anywhere!"

My past had caught up with me! Frankie, whose last name I never did learn, was—like my respectable boss—a piano buff who particularly liked my flashy version of the well-worn standard rag. In San Francisco, he'd call up KTAB during the late-hour "Night Owls" program I hosted, wording his request in a difficult-to-say-"no" manner: "Hey, Glen—if you'll play 'Twelfth Street Rag,' I'll send up a fifth of gin." It was the sort of reward one learned to appreciate in the late twenties and early thirties—especially good pay for three minutes' work.

After my successful "debut" on station KTM, my boss re-scinded his ruling that my accomplishments as a professional entertainer should be kept secret, even though I had no intention of returning to performing other than occasionally. However, Frank Gage, our program director, and I created a comedy act called "Frankie and Johnnie." Frank had an excellent comedy sense, played guitar, piano and trumpet, and we worked well together whether reading from a script or improvising. Actually, the greater part of the half hour program was devoted to our ad libbing.

The program was a hodgepodge of corny jokes, parodies of popular songs, hoked-up instrumental selections and—what seemed to appeal to the listeners most—zany statements of sponsorship and the presentation of parody commercials. Our fictional sponsors included aberrations like "The Whoozit and Howzit Bayou Company—makers of Louisiana Bayous," "The Baldwin Piano and Locomotive Works—manufacturers of grand locomotives and steam pianos," and "Wiggly Spearmint Gum—the gum that wiggles when you choose to chew". And there were commercials for "fur lined bathtubs and mink sinks," "barbed wire suspenders," "Black Owl Cigars, made from fine feathers," and "Whitney's Cotton Gin—the gin with the fuzzy aftertaste".

I describe this program and its contents only because its success resulted in what was probably the most outlandish sponsor relationship known to radio: In 1930 in Los Angeles, a restaurant—especially popular during after-theater hours—was Ptomaine Tommy's. As I recall, there may have been a few tables, but most of the business was at the counter; short order specialties such as hamburgers, waffles, hot dogs, and chili. Tommy was credited with inventing the hamburger "size"—a popular Southern California concoction consisting of an over-sized hamburger patty topped with a generous serving of chili con carne. The name of this specialty was derived from the fact that the patty was of a larger size than that used in a conventional hamburger sandwich. "Si-i-ize!" the waiter or waitress would call to the chef when one was ordered.

One of our time salesmen got the bright idea that Ptomaine Tommy's would make an ideal sponsor for "Frankie and Johnnie". He called upon Tommy, the proprietor, generated his enthusiasm for the idea and clinched his sales pitch with the argument, "If you sponsor this program, it'll pay for itself just with the salesmen from other radio stations who drop in to buy lunch and try to sell you time on *their* stations."

Tommy signed the contract for a thirteen-week run, agreeing to give Frank and me carte blanche in the area of commercials. So far as I know, this series remains the only radio program whose commercials never said one good word about its sponsor's products. We told the audience the restaurant was the best place in town to get ptomaine poisoning; we said the coffee tasted like dishwater, and that Tommy had taken out a patent on his steaks because they were excellent substitutes for rubber heels. Sample dialogue ran like this:

JOHNNIE: I had a meal at Ptomaine Tommy's last night. It was terrible. The onions tasted like baloney, the potatoes tasted like onions, the beans tasted like cabbage, and the cabbage tasted like pickles.

FRANKIE: What are you kicking about? You still got a good meal out of it.

We admonished the listeners: "Don't make fun of Tommy's coffee—you may be old and weak yourself someday," or: "Don't order the hash—Tommy can't remember what's in it."

The climax of the series arrived with our discovery that Tommy had a huge supply of colored postcards which bore a picture of his establishment. Immediately, we decided to play a joke on the audience. We announced that everyone visiting the restaurant (no purchase was necessary) would receive a valuable gift. "Just go in and tell Tommy that Frankie and Johnnie sent you. He'll give you, as a souvenir, the most expensive gift ever given away by a sponsor . . . And it's absolutely free!"

The joke backfired—not because it wasn't successful, but because it was *too* successful. At the end of six weeks, Tommy begged to be let out of his contract. "My God!" he exclaimed, "I can't handle the customers! They're coming in by the hundreds. If it keeps up, I'll have to build another wing on the place or have everybody sore at me!"

Interestingly, Tommy told us that not one person complained

about receiving only a postcard when asking for the gift. The only complaints were about having to wait so long in line to be seated. So the Frankie and Johnnie program lost its sponsor, but remained on the air for a considerable length of time after that with only fictional sponsors and with the satisfaction of knowing we had a loyal following.

2
Crashing the
Hollywood Scene~~~~~~~~~

The Pickwick Broadcasting Corporation eventually returned me to San Francisco as manager of KTAB. I remained until 1933 when the broom of a new top management swept me out along with several of my colleagues. After some free-lancing, I eventually wound up on the staff of KHJ, Los Angeles, where my duties of announcing, writing and producing replaced those of Sylvester (Pat) Weaver who had just been transferred to the Don Lee Broadcasting System's San Francisco station, KFRC, where I had once worked. That was in August, 1934.

In those days, the schedules we maintained were, by today's radio station standards, unbelievable. A sampling of a week of my activities would be something like this:

WRITING: Five five-minute comedy scripts per week. One half-hour drama for the "Don Lee Workshop", an experimental series trying out new techniques.
Collaborating in the writing of (and performing in, on occasion) "The Merrymakers," a one hour comedy-variety program.
Writing continuity for "California Melodies," a half hour musical program for the CBS network which featured the orchestra of

Raymond Paige (later, David Broekman) and guest artists.

Scripts for "Mr. & Mrs. Smith," a fifteen minute, three-a-week situation comedy based on the once popular newspaper comic strip, *Joe and Vi.*

Scripts for "Fooler Dramas," a three-times-per-week series of comedy blackout sketches. Collaborating on continuity for the "Happy-go-Lucky Hour," a half-hour, five-times-per-week daytime comedy-variety show starring Al Pearce and his brother Cal.

PRODUCTION: "California Melodies" (described above). "Mobil Magazine," a weekly half hour program dramatizing news events, feature stories, musical events, etc.

"The Juvenile Revue," a half hour weekly program presenting up-and-coming young talent. (Several of them "up-and came"; among them were two singer-dancer performers— later to become movie stars—Donald O'Connor and Peggy Ryan, pianist Leonard Pennario, the multi-talented Mickey Rooney, and trumpeter Leonard Suess).

"Mr. & Mrs. Smith" (described above).

"Fooler Dramas" (described above).

"The Road to Fame," a weekly half hour program devoted to "discovering" new vocal and instrumental talent.

In addition to these regular duties, there were numerous special assignments. One was producing a Los Angeles cut-in for the Columbia Broadcasting System's "Man on the Street" broadcast. Such programs, as most listeners are aware, gather opinions from interviewees, usually in a location where substantial foot traffic offers an opportunity to poll a variety of people from various walks of life. The KHJ studios were located at an intersection where there was a sufficient number of passers-by for the purpose, so our engineers simply lowered a microphone from an upper story window rather than incur the expense of assigning a mobile unit to another location. In addition to the foot traffic, there were passing automobiles and streetcars.

Announcer Bill Goodwin handled the interviews; an assistant and I snagged the available strollers and led them to the mike. The cut-in went well. The automobiles, streetcars, and traffic-signal bells added excitement and immediacy to the scene. After returning the program to the New York studio at the end of our segment, we headed upstairs to our own studios. The station manager emerged from his office as we stepped from the elevator. Beaming with satisfaction, we awaited his congratulations, for we knew he had been listening in via the loudspeaker near his desk.

Instead, he glowered. "Don't you guys ever pull a stunt like that again! That was a dirty trick—a lousy cheat! We have a responsibility to CBS to do things properly and honestly."

Flabbergasted, we asked for an explanation. It turned out that even with the single condenser microphone we had used, the street traffic, signal bells, and murmur of other voices behind those of the announcer and the interviewees had balanced so perfectly that the station manager had concluded the background sounds had been achieved by means of a sound truck with recordings of crowd voices and traffic noises. It took our entire crew to convince him our realistic city-street ambience had not been faked.

It is apparent in the rundown of my KHJ activities that those of us on the staff were not "clock watchers"; my day often began at 7:30 in the morning and ended at 10:30 in the evening—sometimes with or without an hour or so dinner break, often with time only for a quick sandwich eaten at my desk. On many occasions, such heavy daily schedules ran seven days a week. Pat Weaver, whom I had replaced upon being hired, had run into an embarrassing situation because of his work load:

Thursday was normally Pat's day off, but his schedule was so demanding that he found it necessary, nearly every week, to go to the studio on that day. Pat's mode of transportation was his Model A Ford coupe. Each Thursday morning about ten o'clock as he swung onto Wilshire Boulevard on his way to work, he noticed in his rear view mirror the chauffeur-driven Cadillac limousine of Don Lee, the automobile sales tycoon who was president of the radio network which bore his name.

Sylvester (Pat) Weaver, radio writer and producer, who eventually became President of the National Broadcasting Company.

Pat was embarrassed by the fact that Mr. Lee almost invariably pulled into the radio station's garage just behind him each Thursday, and was well aware that, while arriving late might be the station owner's prerogative, the mid-morning arrival of a full-time employee might be frowned upon. Diffident about approaching Mr. Lee with an explanation, Weaver came up with an ingenious alternative:

The next Thursday, while driving to work and sighting the Don Lee limousine behind him, Pat slowed down so that it was following only a' few feet from his rear bumper. Then he reached around and pulled down the roller shade on the rear window of the Model A. On it, neatly lettered and legible from a considerable distance, was Pat's explanation:

GOING TO WORK
ON DAY OFF

The most influential Hollywood gossip columnist was Louella (Lolly) Parsons, Executive Editor of the Hearst Publications Motion Picture Department. In addition to being featured in the radio series, "Hollywood Hotel," she portrayed herself in the 1937 movie version of the show.

Frances Langford appeared on many successful radio program series, including "Colgate House Party," "Lombardo Land," "Hollywood Hotel," and "Texaco Star Theater." She co-starred with Don Ameche in the popular domestic comedy sketches, "The Bickersons," recorded for Decca Records and was featured in several motion pictures.

Ted Fio Rito and his orchestra were featured on the "Hollywood Hotel" radio series when it was launched on October 5, 1934. Ted is seen here, directing his band and "The Debutantes" trio (l. to r.) Betty Noyes, Marjorie Briggs and Dorothy Hill, and singer Dick Powell who was destined to become a top motion picture and television star. The radio series remained on the air until December 2, 1938.

One of the better known CBS network shows which originated in the KHJ studios during the mid-thirties was the popular "Hollywood Hotel." The regular headliners were the hostess, Louella Parsons, Hearst Syndicate motion-picture columnist, film-musical stars Dick Powell and Frances Langford, and Ted Fio Rito and his Orchestra (later replaced by the orchestra of Raymond Paige). Each week, the hour-long program featured, in addition to the songs of Langford and Powell and selections by the orchestra, interviews with visiting motion-picture stars and radio adaptations of sequences from movies in which they were currently appearing. And, of course, there was the banter and sprinkling of witticisms expected of such sophisticated personalities.

One day, Jack Van Nostrand, a KHJ colleague, and I received

an emergency call from the Hollywood-based Vice-President of the Columbia Broadcasting System. He had just been notified that Campbell Soups, the sponsor of "Hollywood Hotel", had turned down the entire script of the show which was to be broadcast two or three days later. The regular writers either couldn't or wouldn't turn out a completely new script in the short space of time remaining before the air date. If Jack and I could turn out an acceptable script in the brief length of time that was left, we'd be doing CBS a favor which would never be forgotten. We were both flattered and excited by the opportunity offered. Besides, the V.P. said, the pay would be $250. We knew that was less than the regular rate for the "Hollywood Hotel" scripts, but inasmuch as neither Jack nor I were making even $75 a week at the time, the opportunity to make $125 each, on the side, made the project even more exciting!

Not having production duties on that particular evening, we went to work right after dinner. By mid-morning the next day, bleary-eyed from lack of sleep, we delivered a completed script to Mr. Veep who enthusiastically accepted it and showered compliments upon us. Forthwith, the entire script was teletyped to the F. Wallis Armstrong Advertising Agency in Philadelphia, where it received immediate approval. Jack and I had made the Big Time!

Our elation was short-lived: When we went to pick up the $250 check to be split between us, we received instead a check for $125! Asked for an explanation, the Veep replied, "Well, after all, you fellows turned it out overnight. You didn't work all week on it the way the other writers do."

While we questioned the reasoning, we reluctantly accepted the check for half pay; after all, we were moonlighting and we didn't want the CBS Vice-President to make a case of it with the KHJ management. But the real payoff was yet to come.

Because of the pressure upon us to complete the script on such short notice, we had had no time for judicious editing and pruning. Therefore, the script was tremendously over-written. With a modicum of editing and polishing, and a few name changes to accommodate replaced guest stars, someone connected with the "Hollywood Hotel" programs managed to make our script suffice for *two* broadcasts. Our $250 script, purchased for a mere

$125.00, had netted each of us exactly $31.25 for each of two top rated, high-budget, one hour transcontinental radio programs!

No wonder some guys chose the profession of plumbing!

One of the several true geniuses with whom I worked during my many years in radio and television was the Don Lee Broadcasting System's Director of Music, David Broekman. Talented, temperamental, and the possessor of a tremendous ego, he also possessed a very large sense of humor that was sometimes delightful, sometimes touched with malice. One of his delightful gags was inspired by a colleague who had an annoying habit of which he was unaware: While engaged in conversation, if he noticed a fragment of lint on the other man's coat lapel, he would absentmindedly remove it and cast it aside, repeating the gesture several times during a conversation if the lint supply held out.

Once Broekman became aware of this lint-picking idiosyncrasy, he decided to make the most of it. He showed up at the studio one day, gathered most of us about, and revealed his big idea: with a finely pointed brush, he had dabbed a pin head size dot of white paint on the edge of his coat lapel. Then, at intervals throughout the day, he managed to engage the lint-picker in conversation, each time signaling us as he was about to do so. Invariably, the fellow's fingernail was busily trying to remove the white speck while the rest of us struggled to conceal our laughter. Throughout it all, Broekman managed to keep a straight face. I doubt if the lint-picker ever realized he'd provided so much entertainment for so many people while indulging in his impulsive, unconscious pastime.

During a rehearsal of the "California Melodies" program, I heard an orchestral dissonance that bothered me. Broekman was noted for his love of dramatic, unorthodox instrumental effects, and had once told me, "Sometimes I like to crash in with an atonal chord just to make the listener pay attention." I understood, but on occasion, when he got a little too wild, I'd coax him back to reality with the argument, "After all, Dave— if you want to hold an audience, they have to understand what you're doing." In the main, however, I went along with his musical hyperbole and he appreciated it.

In this particular instance, however, it seemed positively ridiculous for the muted brass section to be playing eight bars

of Sousa's march, "The Stars and Stripes Forever," while the
rest of the orchestra played "Diga Diga Doo." After the first
run-through of the number, I left the control room, crossed the
studio to the podium and spoke to Broekman in confidential tones
which could not be overheard by the members of the orchestra:

"Dave," I said in my most diplomatic manner, hoping to
avoid one of his temperamental outbursts in which he might
very well denounce me in front of the orchestra as a musical
moron with no imagination, "I don't think the listeners will
understand why "The Stars and Stripes Forever" is being played
in the middle of "Diga Diga Doo." It's not only dissonant, it
has no reason for being in there. I think it ought to come out."

He looked at me with an expression that implied my musical
stupidity had hurt him to the quick. After a long pause during
which he exhaled an exasperated sigh, he asked, "You don't like
it?"

I braced myself for one of his outbursts as I said, "I'm sorry,
Dave. I don't."

But, instead of pouring a torrent of invective on my head,
he simply shrugged. "Okay," he said, picking up a scrap of
paper from his conductor's stand. Holding the paper aloft to
attract the attention of the musicians, he called out, "Boys—
he. doesn't like it. Take it out!"

With which every man in the brass section removed a similar
scrap of paper from his stand. I'm certain my jaw dropped as
the raucous laughter came from the orchestra. Then it dawned
upon me: Broekman had had his arranger go to all the trouble
of scoring those few bars of "The Stars and Stripes Forever"
and had had the boys in the brass section play them in a malicious
effort to catch me off guard. I've often wondered how my association with the maestro might have continued thereafter had I
fallen into his trap. Then, too, I've often speculated as to what
extent he might have pursued his gag had I not requested removal
of those bastardized eight bars. Would he have brazened it out
and played the dissonant counterpoint to "Diga Diga Doo" over
the CBS coast-to-coast network? Knowing Broekman, I wouldn't
have bet a Gene Krupa paradiddle against it.

In Dave Broekman's orchestra was an accomplished percus-
sionist, Nat Leslie. Dave liked Nat and respected his abilities as

a drummer and composer but, if you think our musical director would pull a practical joke on him in spite of that, you're right; Dave would and did:

Enlisting my cooperation as producer of the program, along with that of the control room engineer and our announcer, Dave arranged to have the studio wall clock set two minutes ahead of the actual hour. This was accomplished just before air time during the orchestra's final five minute break. During the program, Nat's back was toward the wall clock as he played, so that no suspicion was aroused as we began the broadcast two minutes ahead of time—by the clock. As any experienced broadcaster knows, the timings of the programs are double checked with stop watches so, despite the deceitful face of our wall clock, there was little chance of error so far as beginning and ending the program on time was concerned. (A network program must be timed to the second so that each interconnected station will be able to clobber you with local commercials during the station breaks).

It was our custom to time the program so that the *California Melodies* theme closed with a grandiose chord, underlined with a big timpani roll just before the announcer proclaimed, "This is the Columbia Broadcasting System." Broekman would then cue Nat to continue the timpani roll for the thirty second network "fill"—a protection against dead air in the event any of the stations failed to clear on time, or (as happened on rare occasions) had no local announcements to broadcast. On this occasion, the program timed out perfectly; Dave signalled Nat to continue the timpani roll.

As Nat became aware the timp roll was continuing far beyond the usual thirty seconds necessary for the "fill," he glanced quickly over his shoulder at the studio clock. Another minute and a quarter to go! Nat's eyes glazed with panic. Two minutes can seem an eternity to a drummer who must sustain a perfect roll for that length of time. But Nat was a pro: he rolled and rolled and rolled with the sticks with the big, felt heads. Then he began to perspire, literally sweating it out. Intermittently he would glance at the clock as Broekman glared at him in feigned anger whenever the timpani roll gave the slightest indication of faltering. Finally, after 120 seconds, each seeming like a minute, the minute hand of the clock arrived at its destination. Dave lowered his baton panting; Nat slumped into his chair. It took him at least twenty-four hours to see the funny side of it.

Enough of the fun-loving David Broekman. However, before ending this rhythm rhapsody, I'd like to add a coda which has to do with another timpanist: On one occasion, while he'd turned his back on his kettledrums to concentrate on his bass and his snare, a prankster substituted, for his pair of timp sticks, a pair of snare-drum sticks, the ends of which were imbedded into nice, round, jelly doughnuts. Later in the selection, the drummer whirled about from his snare drum, mechanically grabbed the two sticks resting on the kettledrum head and brought them down with a flourish. Splat! And the drumhead was covered with jelly. Even with a name like "Smucker's" it couldn't have been good!

Returning to the rich lore of on-the-air faux pas, we mustn't overlook the sound-effects men. One of the best in the early radio days was a fellow by the name of Lloyd Creekmore, who—to no one's astonishment, I'm sure—spent a considerable amount of time explaining it was "spelled with two "E's—not c-r-e-A-k."

One of Creekmore's most delightful boo-boos occurred during a dramatic program at a moment when the script called for the ringing of a telephone bell. The program was on the air when someone, moving about the studio, inadvertently kicked loose the plug connecting the electrical wall outlet near the floor with the sound effects table. From the control room, I cued "Creek" for the telephone bell. He pressed the proper button, but naturally there was no response. He tried a second time. Then, thinking quickly—but forgetting it was to have been a phone bell and not a doorbell—he gave several rapid knocks on his sound effects door. Then he looked up at me, smiling as smugly as a politician who has just emerged victorious from a brinkmanship contest. Quickly, I pantomimed—one fist at my ear, the other at my mouth—that it should have been a telephone. Still unaware of his blooper, and thinking I was cueing the next sound effect, he promptly lifted the telephone receiver, and the actor who was awaiting *that* cue, said "Hello." I thought it was a rather interesting innovation in communications.

On another occasion, we had trouble during rehearsal with a campfire scene. Clark Gable and his leading lady, Paula Winslowe, were portrayed as being outdoors preparing breakfast. For some reason, the usually effective way of simulating the sound of bacon sizzling in a frying pan—applying a water-soaked cloth to a frying pan on an electric hotplate—didn't quite come off. After unsuccessfully experimenting with other methods, we decided the sound wasn't picking up properly because of the acoustics: the program was being produced on the stage of a theater whose characteristics were different from those of a studio. I suggested to Creek that he buy some bacon and try the actual sound on mike. It worked beautifully.

Later, the audience filled the theater, and soon we were on the air. The romance between Mr. Gable and Miss Winslowe was progressing nicely. The recorded sounds of morning bird songs and the crackling of campfire flames (realistically produced by crinkling cellophane close to the mike) painted a glorious sunrise scene with two people falling in love.

"Do you like bacon?" asked Clark.

"Love it," replied Paula. And Creekmore placed the strips of bacon in the frying pan.

The scene progressed smoothly until the fragrance of the frying bacon wafted out over the audience. We hadn't counted on that! A man and a woman, miles from civilization, in a tender, intimate love scene, were suddenly interrupted by the sound of scores of people reacting to the delicious aroma with a loud "Ummmmmmm!"

The listeners at home couldn't possibly have known what was going on. It probably sounded obscene.

One of my assignments at KHJ was the production of a series of cut-ins for the Gulf Oil Company's program which originated in the New York studios of CBS. The Hollywood cut-in consisted of a monologue by the celebrated cowboy actor and columnist, Will Rogers. Each Sunday afternoon, a small audience gathered in one of the KHJ studios so that Will's performance might be enhanced by timing it to their reactions. He placed his script and an old-fashioned alarm clock on a music stand in front of

Cowboy-actor-author-humorist Will Rogers in a typical onstage pose.

the microphone, stood before it, pushed his hat back from his forehead and stood there chewing gum until he was given the "on the air" cue. Then, tucking the wad in the corner of his mouth with his tongue, he smiled at his small audience and began.

Will Rogers was one of those traditions who could do no wrong: he needled presidents of the United States, goodnaturedly insulted politicians regardless of beliefs or party and, insisting "All I know is what I read in the papers," revealed he knew a great deal more. I recall one delightful broadcast during which his comments startled us because of the jibe Will hurled at his own sponsor. (He had carte blanche so far as his comments were concerned, and none of us were permitted to pass upon his scripts). His remarks occurred shortly after a commercial extolling the Gulf Oil Company's gas stations and the services which they offered motorists. (I quote from memory):

"Whenever I hear the word 'service'," Will began, "I'm always reminded of my days on the farm. When the right time of the year arrived, my Pa would have me take ol' Bossie, our cow, a couple o' miles down the road to a farmer who had a bull for breedin' purposes. 'Take her down and get her serviced,' my Pa would say. It didn't take me long, when I was a kid, to figure out what he meant by 'service.' An' sometimes I think that's just what the oil companies are doing to *us*."

Then, as the audience in the studio rocked with laughter, he looked at me, his eyes twinkling, as though to say, "Don't worry. I can get away with it."

So far as I know, he did, too. Obviously, the Gulf Oil people were just as mesmerized with the Rogers charm as were presidents, politicians, and theater audiences. For those of us who had so often retched beneath the slashes of the blue pencil, it was a day to remember.

~~~~~~~~~~~~~~~~~~~~~~~~

I had been with KHJ and the Don Lee Broadcasting System about two years when CBS purchased radio station KNX from the Los Angeles *Evening Herald-Express*. Naturally, I was interested in moving to the bigger operation, for KNX was to become the key station for originating the network's Hollywood programs. I expressed my desire to Paul Rickenbacher and Charles Vanda,

(l. to r.) The author with Norris (Tuffy) Goff (Lum); assistant writer Betty Boyle; head writer Roswell Rogers; and Chester Lauck (Abner) of the radio series, "Lum 'n' Abner."

both of whom had left KHJ to join KNX as station manager and program director, respectively. Each agreed I should be part of the KNX operation as a writer/producer, but pointed out that CBS had made an agreement with Don Lee that the network would make no more "raids" on the Don Lee personnel. Momentarily frustrated, I was rescued from my predicament by an unexpected opportunity to join the Lord & Thomas advertising agency for a temporary radio-production assignment. Taking advantage of it, I immediately informed Rickenbacher and Vanda that I was no longer a Don Lee employee and, after completing my new assignment, which would require my services from September through December, 1936, I'd be available. Both men assured me they were delighted and that I could count upon being hired by CBS.

At the end of December, I called Rickenbacher and reminded him of the promise he and Vanda had made. Rick hesitated, coughed uncomfortably, talked around the subject for a few moments, then leveled with me:

Ozzie & Harriet's Christmas card shows the Nelson boys, Ricky (l.) and David, at an age when they were too young to read radio scripts. When the series first began, the Nelson boys were portrayed by older, professional child actors.

"Look," he explained, "since Charlie and I talked with you, a situation has developed. We've had a falling out, and are barely on speaking terms. If I hire you, Charlie will fire you. However, I want you to go to work for us, so you call Charlie. If he hires you, *I* won't fire you. But don't let on you've already talked to me."

I breathed a sigh of relief, but kept my fingers crossed. After all, Charlie, knowing I was a friend of Rickenbacher's, might not want to hire me.

My fingers still crossed, I called on Vanda. After a brief chat in his office, he hired me. But there was still more intrigue: "I'll pay you seventy-five dollars a week," he said. I was elated, for, although Lord & Thomas had paid me a hundred dollars a week, my salary at KHJ (including a ten-dollar raise at the end of my first year) had been only sixty dollars. Vanda, of course, didn't sense my elation, explaining apologetically, "That's

Comedian Joe ("Wanna buy a duck?") Penner signs an autograph book for a young fan.

more than anyone else in the program department is making, except me. Now, then, you report to me on all production matters, and to Hector Chevigny on all writing assignments. But don't let Hec know how much you're making, because he's only making forty a week as head of the continuity department."

Now I had two secrets: I couldn't let Vanda know I'd previously talked to Rickenbacher and I couldn't let Chevigny, who was also a good friend of mine, know I was making more than he. Then to compound matters, Charlie said, "I don't know whether you know it, or not, but Paul and I don't get along any more. When Hec has assigned you a desk in continuity, you call Paul and ask him to have a phone installed for you. If *I* have a phone installed, he'll have it disconnected."

We shook hands on our deal. Hec welcomed me with open arms and Paul happily had a phone installed on my desk. Despite the hush-hush aspects of my position, I was off to a good start.

One of my first assignments was to produce a two hour coast-to-coast dedicatory program formally announcing the affiliation of KNX as the CBS-owned key station on the Pacific Coast. The broadcast featured, among other celebrities, vocalist Gertrude Niesen, baritone Igor Gorin, the orchestras of Lud Gluskin and Raymond Paige, Joe Penner ("Wanna buy a duck?"), Bing Crosby, Frances Langford, and—their first appearance on any stage together in their long careers—Al Jolson and Eddie Cantor joining in duets on songs each had made famous, from "Mammy" and "Sonny Boy" to "Tomatoes are Cheaper" and "It You Knew Susie Like I Knew Susie".

For some time previous to the KNX-CBS special broadcast, there had existed an icy standoffishness between Jolson and Cantor. Apparently contributing to the ill feeling between them was the fact that although Eddie Cantor had starred in the Broadway musical-comedy production *Whoopee* in 1927, Samuel Goldwyn had chosen Al to star in the film production. To that end, in 1930, Goldwyn summoned him to Hollywood. The following story concerning that episode in the lives of the two entertainers was told to me by Jolson himself:

While in Hollywood, prior to the filming of *Whoopee*, Al and Sam Goldwyn played quite a bit of golf together. According to Al, Sam—otherwise a man of considerable integrity—couldn't

Rosemary Clooney and Bing Crosby chat during a rehearsal break. The occasion was her appearance on one of the famous annual "Christmas Sing with Bing" radio shows.

In this picture, the famous entertainer, Al Jolson, seems about to burst into a rendition of his most popular song, "Mammy." Al performed often in radio and had successful runs on two series: "Shell Chateau" (NBC, 1935–36) and "Al Jolson at the Trocadero" (CBS, 1936–39). The latter show was also known as "Tuesday Night Party."

bear to lose and was habitually lowering the number of strokes per hole as he entered them on his score card. One day, Jolson again caught him in the act. Having admonished Goldwyn on several previous occasions, Jolson became extremely annoyed. "Sam," he threatened, "if you cheat like that once more, I'm gonna pee on your leg."

Goldwyn, shrugging off the threat as a mere joke, waited until he'd played another couple of holes, then once more committed his peccadillo. Jolson unbuttoned his fly and followed through on his threat.

"All over one leg of his gray flannel slacks," Jolson laughed as he concluded his anecdote. "And that's why Sam canceled my contract and put in Cantor as the star of *Whoopee*."

There would be more cloak-and-dagger operations at KNX. For example, an argument over a script spawned one situation that might have been a sketch in a musical revue except that the "cast" was comprised of broadcasting professionals rather than comedians:

Lud Gluskin, who had been a CBS staff musical director in New York, had been transferred to Hollywood to supervise the CBS musical activities on the Pacific Coast and also to conduct special programs like Chevigny's award-winning "White Fires" dramatic series, as well as his own weekly musical feature, "On the Air with Lud Gluskin." Hec Chevigny had been assigned to write the continuity (the announcer's introductions to the musical selections) for the "On the Air" programs. Unfortunately, Hec—who was actually a more proficient dramatist and all-around writer* than any of the rest of us—did not have a musical background. Therein lies the motivation for the intrigue which followed:

Paul Rickenbacher called me into his office one day, instructed his secretary that he was not to be interrupted, closed the door of his office, then *molto mysterioso*, swore me to secrecy.

---

* In addition to his radio work, which was versatile enough to include soap operas as well as mature drama, Hector Chevigny turned out such lasting books as *Lord of Alaska, North to Empire*, and *My Eyes Have a Cold Nose*.

"Lud's dissatisfied with Hec's writing," he said. "So I want you to take over his job of writing 'On the Air'."

"Why the sneaky stuff?" I asked.

Paul grinned. "It's like this . . . Lud went into Charlie Vanda's office, complained about Hec's scripts, and asked that another writer be assigned. Charlie refused. Lud got upset and to emphasize how he felt, told Charlie, 'Hell—I can write better than that, myself!' Well, Charlie got sore and said, 'Then go ahead and do it!' Having had his bluff called, Lud stormed out of Charlie's office and called me."

"So I'm the goat," I commented.

"Not goat," countered Rickenbacher, "*ghost*. Lud has to save face, and he can't write a script, so you're his ghost writer."

That was how it began. There followed many weeks of devious maneuvers; after Lud had selected the numbers for his program and had laid out the order in which they would be played on the air, he'd call me on the phone. Then, whenever I could gracefully get away from my desk, which was across a narrow aisle from Chevigny's, I would sneak upstairs to Gluskin's office. He would bolt the door, and we'd discuss the program in low, guarded voices. After my day's work was ended, I'd take my notes home with me and type far into the night until each script was completed. On the following day, I'd surreptitiously report back to Lud and—again behind a locked door—we'd go over the script, make any necessary revisions, and Lud would personally take "his" script to the mimeograph department.

I was in Vanda's office several weeks after the start of this smuggling operation, when during the discussion of another program in which Gluskin was involved, Charlie brought up the subject of "On the Air": "You know," he said, "that Lud's an amazing character. I've known him for years—knew him back in New York—and I never knew he could write."

"Write?" I asked, feigning innocence.

"Yeah. You know, he came in here a few weeks ago, beefing about Hec's scripts. He wanted me to put another writer on the show, but I got stubborn and said I wouldn't. Lud got sore and said he could write the scripts better himself. I told him, 'Go ahead, for all I care.' "

Edmund (Tiny) Ruffner, the nearly-seven-feet-tall announcer of Al Jolson's CBS series, is seen here with Harry Einstein, who became famous as Jolson's stooge, "Parkyakarkas," with his comedic Greek accent.

Milton Berle, in 1937, when he was first attracting nationwide attention as featured comedian on "The Gillette Community Sing" radio series. Others on the show were Wendell Hall, "The Redheaded Music Maker"; the vocal team of Billie Jones and Ernie Hare; Eileen Barton ("Jolly Gillette, the Sponsor's Daughter") and Andy Sanella's orchestra.

"And—" I prompted.

Charlie shook his head in disbelief. "He called my bluff . . . And you know something? The sonofabitch *can* write!"

Long after we had both departed KNX, I told Chevigny what had been going on behind his back. His astonishment gave way to laughter. "I *wondered* about those scripts. I figured he must have had a ghost writer, but I would never have guessed it was you. If I had, it would have been okay with me. I was just teed off at the time because I didn't think he should have been able to write that well after Charlie had called his bluff."

The experience I gained at KNX was invaluable, for it gave me an insight into big time network operations and put me in contact with professionals who contributed to the honing of my own skills. With some, I have had continuing professional associations; others became long-time friends.

In addition to the several shows I personally produced for local release, I was CBS contact producer on such network favorites as "The Park Avenue Penners" (Joe Penner, Dick Ryan who portrayed Joe's English butler, Jimmy Grier's orchestra, high-voiced Gene Austin of "My Blue Heaven" fame, and announcer Jack Wheeler); "Al Jolson at the Trocadero" (Jolson, Sid Silvers, Patsy Flick, Martha Raye, Harry Einstein with his portrayal of the comedic Greek character, Parkyakarkas, Victor Young's orchestra, and the six-foot six-inch tall announcer, "Tiny" Ruffner); the "Original Gillette Community Sing" (rising star Milton Berle, the comedy/singing team of Billy Jones and Ernie Hare, Wendell Hall, the ukelele-playing "Red-Headed Music Maker" of *It Ain't Gonna Rain No Mo'* fame, Eileen Barton, then a child singing star billed as "Jolly Gillette, the Sponsor's Daughter," comedian Tommy Mack, Andy Sanella's orchestra, and announcer Dan Seymour). I served also as CBS producer of Hector Chevigny's "White Fires" (dramatic vignettes from the lives of people driven to success through consuming inspiration).

My days at KNX were exciting ones. I had intended to remain there as long as CBS would have me, unaware that an even more exciting opportunity would soon come my way.

3

The Big Time

Pat Weaver, whom I succeeded at KHJ, had eventually become employed by one of the nation's leading advertising agencies, Young & Rubicam, Inc. (Still later, Pat became President of the National Broadcasting Company). The agency, headquartered in New York City, had suddenly found it necessary to enlarge its Hollywood staff because of an unexpectedly stepped-up radio production schedule. The offices had originally been established as agency production headquarters for the "Jack Benny Program," but with only short notice, Hollywood network originations also included "The Packard Mardi Gras" (sponsored by the Packard Motor Car Company) which starred comedians Walter O'Keefe and Charlie Butterworth, tenor Lanny Ross, soprano Florence George, Raymond Paige and his Orchestra, and announcer Don Wilson; "The Burns & Allen Show"; "The Phil Baker Show"; and a new entry, "Silver Theater."

Upon Weaver's recommendation, four of his former KHJ colleagues were engaged by the agency. I was one of them. My assignment was to produce "Silver Theater", a series featuring glamorous guest stars in original radio dramas by top writers and, as host, veteran stage and screen actor Conrad Nagel, who was billed as "director." (Using a well-known personality to "front" a program was not an unusual practice in radio. Although at least three different competent radio director/producers had been responsible for the excellent "Lux Radio Theater"

59

series, the general public never questioned the billing of "Our director, Mr. Cecil B. De Mille," despite the fact he was busy making motion pictures while the "Lux Radio Theater" rehearsals were in progress).

I joined Young & Rubicam in June, 1937, well ahead of the "Silver Theater" series which was to be launched on October 3rd. However, there was plenty to do. There was much planning of program details—format, selecting a musical director, picking stories for radio adaptation, auditioning actors for the role of host (Nagel was selected from these auditons), reserving a theater from which the program could be broadcast before an audience, hiring a staff writer for the adaptations, selecting a musical theme, and canvassing talent agencies for guest star availabilities. And, of course, there was the necessity of figuring a budget breakdown so that the sponsor's appropriation for the first thirteen week cycle might be properly averaged out.

It was eventually decided the first guest star would be Claudette Colbert whose name was still glowing with her successes in *It Happened One Night, Imitation of Life* and *Private Worlds.* All of us were delighted upon learning she had signed the contract to not only star on the opening broadcast of the series, but to lend her endorsement to the product in a full page, four color advertisement in *Life* magazine. Then it happened:

For some reason known only to Miss Colbert and her agent, she suddenly decided she didn't like the story she had approved upon signing the contract. She wanted out, and no reasoning or coaxing could make her change her mind. A contract is a contract, of course, but trying to work with an unhappy actress or actor can be as frustrating as trying to row a leaky canoe while bailing out the water. The advertising agency and the sponsor agreed to "let her off the hook".

This, however, opened a whole keg of nails: we were now into the month of July and *Life,* having a national magazine's usual three month deadline for advertising insertions, was already rolling the presses. Therefore, the agency had to buy up the complete run of the four color pages and plead with the publishers to hold the presses until a substitution could be made. Hurried negotiations were launched to obtain the services of the talented Rosalind Russell. Miss Russell's name was not then as

*Actress Claudette Colbert, star of the movie. "It Happened One Night,"
as she appeared during a radio show rehearsal in 1950.*

In the foreground, rehearsing for a "Silver Theater" radio performance, are James Stewart and Rosalind Russell. The orchestra conductor is Felix Mills. At his right are producer Glenhall Taylor and announcer John Conte. At the microphone on the right is the program's host, Conrad Nagel.

big as Colbert's, but she was fresh in the minds of the public because of her two recent successes, *Craig's Wife* and *Night Must Fall.* Top photographer Paul Hesse was hired, a portrait made, the proofs rushed to her home for approval, and airmailed special delivery to *Life.*

Meanwhile, on Miss Russell's recommendation, we hired screen writer Grover Jones to create a story line for a four part drama (one half hour to be broadcast on each of four successive Sundays) to be called "First Love." This was one of those rare instances in which the story was written to fit the title, for the International Silver Company was introducing a new sterlingware pattern under that name. True Boardman, a skilled radio writer, was hired to adapt the story to the medium. Also at Miss Russell's suggestion, we employed James Stewart

One of radio's most prolific and skilled authors, True Boardman wrote numerous scripts for "Silver Theater" and Pat O'Brien's series, "Rexall Theater". Boardman is also an accomplished actor.

as her leading man. Jimmy wasn't a big name at the time, but he had made lasting impressions in some of the first films he had made for Metro-Goldwyn Mayer and his distinctive voice made for great identification in radio.

I was lucky. "Silver Theater" became a success with its very first broadcast. The reviews of radio columnists and the trade papers heaped praise upon Roz, Jimmy, the Boardman/Jones writing, and the music of Felix Mills' orchestra. "Silver Theater Sure Hit," read the headline in the *Hollywood Reporter*. The **review stated, ". . . remarkable for its finish, its fine balance** of theatrical values, and for ingratiating performances by Rosalind Russell and James Stewart in leading roles. . . . The setting was ideal for Grover Jones, and he fitted the play with just enough hokum to give it maximum appeal of the popular pot of gold at the end of the rainbow variety . . ."

"Grover Jones, Vet Film Writer, Shows How Radio Scripts Should Be Written," was weekly *Variety's* headline. The review continued with ". . . although the acting and direction rate complimentary mention, it is the script that professionally arouses admiration . . ." *Variety* agreed with the "hokum" reference in the *Hollywood Reporter*, stating, "This is standard boy-meets-girl stuff which keeps it universal just as the writer keeps the two main characters squarely center stage."

Grover was delighted with the statements that it was "hokum" and "standard boy-meets-girl-stuff." This was the kind of writing that had been his throughout a career which had produced a long list of successes.* "I've written 365 screenplays," he boasted, "and not one word of literature. But, goddammit, I'm commercial!" Fortunately for "Silver Theater," Boardman, too, was "commercial." After all, while the story was the creation of Jones, the script was actually Boardman's who, incidentally, went on to become a top writer in radio and television.

Except for a hiatus—the result of a recession during the 1937–1938 broadcast season—"Silver Theater" remained on the air for several years. I launched the post-recession cycle of programs in October, 1938, with Fredric March as the first guest

---

* Among Grover Jones' many successful screenplays were *Souls at Sea, Little Shepherd of the Hills, Abe Lincoln in Illinois, Trail of the Lonesome Pine,* and *Lives of a Bengal Lancer.*

star and continued as producer until the summer of 1941. The production duties were subsequently taken over by the well-known English actress, Edna Best, Ted Bliss and Rupert Lucas. Eventually, Conrad Nagel was replaced by John Loder, who was also billed as director. When one actively participates in a weekly radio series for nearly four years, working with many writers and scores of prominent guest stars, amusing incidents occur with such frequency that it would be impossible to recall more than a mere fragment of the mental montage they eventually become. Although I never attempted to record them as they occurred, the following anecdotes recount a few "Silver Theater" memories:

Grover Jones was gifted with a deep insight into human behavior, a keen sense of humor, and a way with words. During our story conferences, he garrulously rambled along spouting ideas as True Boardman and I reached out, every now and then, to grab one for the script. During one such session, he abruptly quit talking, paused, then looked at us with dancing eyes and said, "Good God, I'm loquacious! Isn't it fortunate I'm interesting?"

Another anecdote concerns "Silver Theater's" first star, Rosalind Russell. One evening, those of us assembled about the conference table in the Young & Rubicam Hollywood offices were becoming restless because Roz was tardy. But only a few minutes later the door burst open and she flounced in, breathless and apologetic. "I'm sorry," she said, "but I was trying to find my cigarette lighter."

I thought that a feeble excuse for being late, but her explanation evoked not only my forgiveness but a hearty laugh:

"I was driving in from Beverly Hills when I decided to have a cigarette. After I lit it, I threw my lighter out the car window —right in the middle of the Sunset Strip. So I stopped and went looking for it." That, I suggest, falls into the category of the old joke about the absent-minded professor who scratched his waffles and poured maple syrup on his mosquito bites.

One of our guest stars—at that time recently risen to stardom—was John Garfield. A warm, sincere fellow whose talents had been channeled away from potential juvenile delinquency and into acting by the noted educator, Angelo Patri, John, while

Popular in both films and radio, John Garfield quickly rose to stardom but his career was all too brief; he died at the age of 39.

enjoying his stature as a motion-picture celebrity, made no attempt to draw a curtain over his past. Typical of his appreciation of both his earlier years and his life as a screen luminary is the vignette he himself described:

"I was having lunch with some friends in '21' in New York shortly after I'd made my first movie, when I noticed a good-looking girl at a table close by. She'd stare at me, then lean over to whisper to the others at her table. They'd look at me, whisper back, and eye me some more. I figured they'd seen my film and were all excited over being so close to a movie star in this classy restaurant. I was feeling pretty important, but I tried to look modest and pretend not to notice—although I sneaked a peek in that direction several times. Finally, as we were leaving, she called out to me: 'I know you!' She was now even more excited.

"I smiled and thanked her. I tried to act calm, but I admit I was thrilled over being recognized as a movie star. 'You're Jules Garfinkle—P. S. 30!' she said. She knew me, all right."

"Silver Theater" was broadcast from the stage of the radio theater in Hollywood's Columbia Square, which seated just under a thousand people. Usually, nothing untoward occurred but, on occasion, the unexpected did happen. Such as:

Between the acts of "Silver Theater", the sponsor's commercials were interpolated. Sometimes they were delivered by the program's announcer, sometimes they were dramatized, or sometimes read by a "commercial voice." On this particular day, International Silver Company's commercials plugged the new silverware pattern, "First Love." One of those commercials was delivered by commercial-voice actress Paula Winslowe, a member of our small "stock company" of versatile performers who handled everything from bit parts to starring roles. In the commercial, she portrayed a young bride.

Following the musical "curtain" at the end of the first act, Paula walked to center stage, stood before the mike, and delivered her opening lines: "I am a June bride. My silverware pattern is International Silver's exquisite 'First Love'."

She read the speech beautifully but, after the first five words, a big wave of laughter scudded through the studio audience. I'm sure there were thousands of puzzled listeners in homes

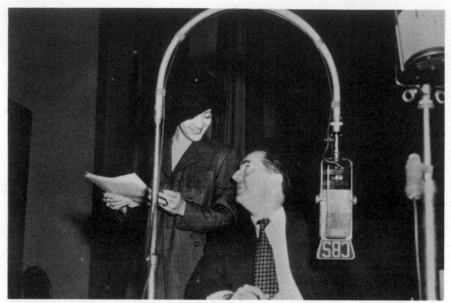

One of radio's most versatile and popular actresses, Paula Winslowe, is seen here with MGM star, William Powell, during a "Silver Theater" rehearsal. When the photographer asked Powell to pose, the actor said, "Come on Paula—they want to take our picture. It's early Sunday morning and we're all smiles and no heart."

from coast to coast, for the line, "I am a June bride," is about as *un*funny a line as a copywriter could create. What none of us had thought of during the commercial rehearsal was that Paula, portraying the June bride, was bulgingly pregnant!

David Niven was one of our many guest stars, and as his books *The Moon's a Balloon* and *Bring on the Empty Horses* attest, he is an anecdotist of no mean ability. One of his many delightful stories has to do with his then employer, Samuel Goldwyn. It was the Goldwyn Studio's policy, when granting its contract employees permission to perform on radio, to demand one-half of the fee received by the player. When David mentioned to us that half of what we were paying him would go to Goldwyn, it immediately recalled to his mind a prank he had played on his boss:

David Niven: actor, raconteur, author, and a connoisseur of the better things in life, including martinis. He was one of the most debonair men to appear upon the stage, in films, and in radio and television.

David had appeared as a guest of Bing Crosby's on "Kraft Music Hall," a stint for which he was paid $2500. As a token perquisite in addition to the actors' fees, it was Kraft's practice to deliver to each of their homes a large, circular wicker tray of packaged cheeses, samples of the sponsor's products. Upon receiving his $2500 check, David wrote his own check for $1250. Then, with a large sharp knife, he cut the array of cheeses in half—tray and all—and had one half delivered to Sam Goldwyn along with the check. "The old boy didn't seem to think it at all amusing," said Niven, crinkling the corners of his eyes with that famous smile of his.

Just prior to his appearance on "Silver Theater," Niven, with the Englishman's typical love of country and sense of duty, had enlisted in his old Scottish regiment which was ultimately to be in the thick of combat in World War II. He told us it had been a difficult task to inform Goldwyn of his decision. "After all, the old boy had been awfully good to me," said David. However, after he had done so, Goldwyn not only understood, but commended him for his action.

"A day or so later," said Niven, "Sam called me into his office and read a farewell letter he had written to me. It was very touching—actually, a beautiful letter. I sat there across the desk from him, all misty-eyed. Then he buzzed his secretary on the intercom and had her send in the studio's public relations chief. Sam was sincerely sad over my leaving. Tears were trickling down his cheeks as he handed a carbon copy of the letter to the chap, but he said, 'Here's something I've written to Davey. I want you should let it leak out to the press.'"

I directed many radio programs starring Pat O'Brien. A sentimental Irishman, Pat was delighted with a half hour original drama True Boardman had written with him in mind. In the play, Pat portrayed an American mobster of Irish parents who returned to the Ireland of his childhood on a sentimental journey. The other two protagonists were his former sweetheart and his boyhood pal who had become a priest. As the story progressed, Pat attended a rollicking "come-all-ye" and, as he danced with the girl, he became once again smitten with her. An obligatory sentimental scene ensued.

During rehearsal, as Pat guided her outdoors, there was the

Actor Pat O'Brien, photographed during a radio show rehearsal. In addition to his countless guest appearances on dramatic and comedy shows, Pat starred in his own radio series, "Rexall Theater," sharing star billing with Lynn Bari (1947) and Virginia Bruce (1948).

Comedian Red Skelton (center) confers with director Glenhall Taylor during a rehearsal. The then Mrs. Skelton, Edna, is at the left.

sound effect of a door closing behind them. Simultaneously, the volume level of the laughter and music was abruptly lowered to indicate the transition from indoors to outdoors. It worked perfectly but, as we got into the outdoor scene (the out-of-doors-at-night ambience simulated by recorded bird sounds and the chirping of crickets) it suddenly occurred to me the scene should be technically correct. I flipped the talk-back switch and interrupted the sequence:

"Pat," I said, "I need some technical advice. Do they have crickets in Ireland?"

Without a pause, he replied, "Yes. But they're all Protestants."

So that the unenlightened reader doesn't remain in suspense, it should be stated that, after the laughter died down, we learned that the background of our scene was correct: there *are* crickets in Ireland.

The list of quips and horseplay is as long as the roster of stars who guested on the "Silver Theater" series. Red Skelton starred in a half hour version of "Eskimo Fever." When, in one scene, he slipped on the ice and fell, the home listeners

Robert Montgomery became famous as a leading man in many MGM motion pictures and was a favorite of directors of radio dramas. He added to his fame as host-producer of his own television series, "Robert Montgomery Presents," and as the father of Elizabeth Montgomery who starred in the TV series, "Bewitched."

Bandleader and host of "The College of Musical Knowledge," Kay Kyser, is at the microphone with his vocalist-wife, Georgia Carroll.

Lovely Ginny Simms was bandleader Kay Kyser's vocalist in the old radio days; she was featured in Kay's "College of Musical Knowledge".

heard a suitable sound effect and also a burst of hilarious laughter. The sound effect came from the sound man flopping limply down on a table top; the laughter came from the audience as a result of Red's irrepressible impulse to visually brighten up the scene by pretending to slip, then somersaulting over the footlights to land on his back on the floor of the auditorium.

In a broad travesty on an oldfashioned, villian-still-pursues-her type of melodrama, the distingushed Robert Montgomery, concealing his intentions from the rest of us, managed to surprise everyone—including the theater audience. At one point, the script called for him to leave his house and go out into a driving snow storm. The action was depicted by the sound of a door creaking open and a simultaneous snarl of wintry blizzard produced by a wind machine. As the door opened and the wind blasted loudly, Bob reached into his coat pocket and pulled forth a large handful of bits of white paper which he tossed high above his head. The do-it-yourself snow storm produced the biggest laugh of the program.

Kay Kyser, the band-leader "president" of the famous "College of Musical Knowledge," who appeared on "Silver Theater" with his vocalist, Ginny Simms as his costar, also contrived a private gag to pull on us and the audience: just before the pre-broadcast warmup ended, two uniformed CBS pages—one in each aisle of the theater—came from the rear toward the stage carrying sheaves of newspapers, and calling out, "Extra! . . . Extra paper!" Each page held aloft a copy for all to see. The bold, black headline read:

KYSER & SIMMS
RETARD RADIO 10 YEARS!

(Kay had gone to a Hollywood Boulevard joke store the previous day, and had the phony front-page headlines printed).

To the layman, producing a half-hour program once each week may seem like sailing before a friendly breeze on a smooth sea. I can recall my mother, who used to listen to my programs nearly every Sunday, once asking me, "What do you do the rest of the week?" For the reader who may wonder, the following may give a fairly good idea of what went on between Sundays:

We can dismiss Monday quite easily: that was usually my day off. Tuesday through Friday were office days during which

A rare "get-together": (l. to r.) Bandleader Kay Kyser: his vocalist, Ginny Simms; comedienne Charlotte Greenwood; actress/syndicated columnist, Hedda Hopper; actor John Barrymore; and Penny Singleton, better known to radio and film fans as "Blondie".

I read story ideas, interviewed actors, agents, writers, dictated correspondence—teletypes, letters, and memoranda—worked on script rewrites with the show's writers who had turned out first drafts at their homes or their own offices, worked on budget problems, and handled numerous other business details. The casting of each show also had to be done during those office hours. On occasion we had daytime rehearsals, but the normal routine called for evening sessions because of the studio commitments of our stars.

For the show, which originated in Hollywood at 3:00 in the afternoon for a 6:00 P. M. release on the East Coast, rehearsals usually began on Wednesday night. This meant a session from about 8:00 until 10:00 or 11:00, after which the writer, the assistant producer and I would get busy with the necessary rewrites. On Thursday night a second rehearsal was held, and on Friday night a dress rehearsal at which the musical conductor

Going over the script prior to a "Silver Theater" rehearsal are director Glenhall Taylor (standing) and (l. to r., seated) an unidentified actor; Joseph Kearns (later to become the zany guardian of Jack Benny's vault with its creaking door and rattling chains); actress Paula Winslowe; sound-effects man, Ray Erlenborn; star Ginger Rogers; and writer True Boardman. Standing behind Boardman is the show's host, Conrad Nagel.

would be present, his pianist representing the full orchestra which would report on Sunday. On that day, the rehearsal was held in two sessions—one in the morning and another after a lunch break. During the lunch break for the actors, sound men and others on the program, the script was given a final going-over for corrections, improved clarity and timing. Following the dress rehearsal, complete with orchestra, sound effects, cast and announcer, the script would receive its final polish and adjustments for split-second timing. Including desk work, rehearsals, miscellaneous details and the actual broadcast, the half hour show added up to a work week totaling at least sixty hours—more often than not, eighty.

One practice which we found very helpful to everyone con-

Here are two of "Silver Theater's" favorite and most charismatic guest stars, Brian Aherne (l.) and Cary Grant.

Screen star William Powell and Gracie Allen, George Burns' famous partner, perform on "Command Performance". These popular programs were recorded in Hollywood and broadcast around the world to American Armed Forces during the Second World War.

cerned with the series was that of recording the Friday night dress rehearsal. Following that session, the stars of the program would join us in the Young & Rubicam conference room and listen to their performances. The writers and I would offer suggestions for improvement and, of course, would accommodate our guests by making any reasonable changes which would aid them on Sunday.

It was interesting to observe the various reactions of the actors who listened to the playback of their performances. Brian Aherne, for example, suddenly rose from his chair after only ten minutes of listening. Picking up his hat and placing it on his head, he commented upon his performance thus: "I can't stand listening to the bounder. He's so bloody British." And he left.

During one of the playback sessions, Jimmy Stewart was apparently listening to himself for the first time. Turning to us with a look of amazement, he said in his famous drawl, "Why do I sound so goddam slow?"

William Powell was especially delightful to work with during these sessions. His quick wit and perception of dramatic values contributed to a creative knack often lacking in the average performer who may know when something is wrong for him, but is at a loss to suggest a remedy. Bill's serious lines, as well as his quips, were often better because of his touch. He used to stay until the end of such sessions, even though some lasted until two or three in the morning. Even in his everyday conversation he was quite inventive. On one occasion, as a couple of us passed his table in a restaurant, he was sipping a before-dinner martini. He raised his glass to us and, smiling, extended an invitation: "Care to join me in studying some miniatures?"

Then there was the time when Bill guested on one of our programs shortly after recuperating from a serious intestinal operation. When asked about his experience, he replied, "The hospital wasn't much different than the studio. Only instead of a length of film, the doctor would hold up a strip of intestine to the light, look at it and say, 'This sequence has got to go,' and snip it off. Then he'd do it again. And, just like at MGM, half of me wound up on the cutting room floor."

Undoubtedly, the movie personality who triggered the most

A Sunday-afternoon crowd lines up in anticipation of Carole Lombard's "Silver Theater" appearance at CBS' Columbia Square on Sunset Boulevard in Hollywood. Such crowds were commonplace during radio's heyday.

laughs during her several guestings on "Silver Theater" was Carole Lombard. Stunningly beautiful, this talented and versatile actress had perfected her art by working diligently at everything she did, whether it was the low comedy of her Mack Sennett days (it was Sennett who changed her name from Jane Peters to Carole Lombard), the high comedy of *Nothing Sacred*, or the deeply moving drama of *They Knew What They Wanted*.

Carole excelled at comedy. It is probably accurate to state that since her passing, no other actress has equaled her skill in the projection of sophisticated humor. (This is not to detract from the likes of Lucille Ball, Carol Burnett, and Bea Arthur, whose talents are considerable, but who flourish in a different metier). In addition to the exquisite timing of her performances, she possessed a delightful sense of humor and a highly creative sense of comedy—especially in contriving pranks.

I recall her arrival at one rehearsal late in 1939: Carole

had just seen a preview of *Gone With the Wind*. She had been tremendously impressed, as were the millions of moviegoers who would later see it. Her enthusiasm was bubbling over; she had to tell us all about it. And, though she was married to Clark Gable at the time, she suddenly became his greatest fan. "Paw is sensational!" she exclaimed. "You know—he's really the king! . . . That's what he is—king!" (Later, to many, it would become Gable's nickname).

Some time after that she told us, "You know—after the *Gone With the Wind* premiere in Atlanta and all that publicity, Paw got to strutting around—too big for his britches." Then, breaking into laughter, she added, "But I fixed him, the big ham!"

She recounted how she had hired an ambulance and had picked a time when she was certain Clark would be at home. Following her instructions, the emergency vehicle, siren whining, had wheeled into the driveway at the Gables' Encino ranch and pulled to a stop. The siren was moaning its last as Gable opened the front door of their home. Already the ambulance attendants were on their way toward the steps, carrying between them a blanket-covered stretcher. Clark was completely flabbergasted and stood, open-jawed, as the men with their burden stopped before him.

"What *is* this?" he demanded.

"Take a look and see," suggested Carole.

Gingerly, Clark lifted a corner of the blanket. Then, as it revealed nothing, he pulled it farther back. There on the stretcher was a huge, cured ham which Carole had purchased at the supermarket.

"I just didn't want his head to get too big," she explained to us.

Clark loved it whenever Carole pulled one of her pranks on him. Granted, the stresses of a two-ego family must have caused difficulties at times, but it was obvious to their friends they were made for each other. As readers of movie columns and fan magazines must know, Clark was an inveterate huntsman. Deer season, duck season, or any other season that called for marksmanship and a chance to get together with his cronies beckoned Clark as surely as a moose horn lures a moose. Carole

Clark Gable was an inveterate hunter and fisherman. In this rare shot, he is seen "roughing it" as he unloads his gear from his station wagon.

accompanied him on these safaris whenever she was free of studio commitments, and demeaned herself to the ritual of outdoor hardships—water and wind, rising before dawn, outdoor bathroom facilities, camping out . . . the works.

Arriving at one of our rehearsals, she said she'd been with Clark on a two week hunting expedition in Mexico, living in and out of their station wagon. Her description of the junket was a narrative of hardships: bumpy roads, miserable sleeping conditions, makeshift meals, and whatnot. I couldn't visualize her in waders and mackinaw clutching a double-barrelled shotgun, and asked her if she really liked the hunting life. "I hate it!" she said, "But if I don't do it with him, you can bet some other broad will. And I'm not going to give any of 'em a chance!"

Myron Selznick, brother of *Gone With the Wind* producer David O., and at that time Hollywood's biggest talent agent, was the butt of two of Carole's ingenious gags:

With Myron representing her, Carole's career had steadily

risen; their relationship was a happy one. There came a time when the contract between them was to be renewed. Selznick called Carole on the phone and discussed it with her. Satisfied with the terms, Carole told him to drop the contract in the mail for her to sign. As was his custom, Selznick forwarded the agency's standard printed form, an "X" indicating the line for her signature. Several days later, the documents, duly executed by Carole, arrived on his desk. He affixed his signature and returned her copy to her.

Weeks went by. Patiently, Carole awaited the proper moment for her coup. Finally, she telephoned him. "Where's my share of the profits?" she demanded.

"What do you mean?" asked Selznick, puzzled.

"The check for all that money you owe me," she replied.

Bewildered, Selznick requested an explanation. He got it: Carole informed him that, according to the terms of their contract, she was entitled to a 50% share of the profits of the Myron Selznick Agency. "Read your contract," she instructed.

She stayed on the line while he got it out of the file. When he got back on the phone, the contract before him on his desk, she gave him the page number and pinpointed the paragraph in which the terms were stipulated. He read and gasped.

Carole had taken the contract he had sent her to a printer who had duplicated it exactly—both as to typography and wording—except that, in the paragraph in question, Carole had had the printer insert, without noticeably changing the appearance of it, a sentence by which Selznick guaranteed to share his profits with her on a 50–50 basis.

"I've got my copy right here, Myron," she said. "It's got your signature on it."

He, of course, recognized it as a prank, but his laugh was an uneasy one. "You always told me to read every word of any contract before signing it," she reminded him. "I just wanted to see if you followed your own advice."

A proper contract between them was forthwith signed, but it is reasonable to assume that thereafter Mr. Selznick scrutinized contracts more carefully, even though they might be the official, printed forms of his own agency.

Selznick's elegant Beverly Hills establishment included the

luxury of a private bathroom adjacent to his office. While it was a great convenience for him, Carole often found it extremely inconvenient. On numerous occasions when she'd call him on important business in the morning, he'd be unavailable. And often she waited for what seemed an interminable length of time before he'd return her call. On one such occasion when she impatiently called a second time, she was informed he was *still* in his private bathroom.

Carole's friends relished her use of four letter words. On this day, her agent's continued unavailability in her moment of need flushed out a bevy of them:

"What in hell does he do in there for so goddamned long?" Carole asked Selznick's secretary.

"He sits there and reads the trade papers while having his 'morning's morning'," replied the secretary euphemistically.

"You mean the sonofabitch sits in the can for a whole hour reading the goddamn *Variety* and *Hollywood Reporter*?" asked Carole. "Can't you do anything about it?"

"I'm afraid I can't, Miss Lombard."

Carole determined *she* would do something about it.

Enlisting the cooperation of the secretary and the switchboard operator, she made elaborate plans. Engaging the services of a studio sound technician, she had him install a loudspeaker in an inconspicuous position in the bathroom where Selznick, seated in his cubicle, could clearly hear it. The loudspeaker, in turn, was connected to the switchboard just off the reception room of the offices. The following morning Selznick's secretary, delighted to be in on the gag, called Carole at her home and informed her that King Myron was heading for his throne in the bathroom.

Carole hung up, waited long enough to allow him to be seated and then called back, asking for Mr. Selznick. The switchboard operator, having been alerted that this was the moment, plugged in the jack that would connect the actress with the loudspeaker in the john.

By this time, the male members of the Selznick staff had been alerted and, with the bathroom door ajar, were peering in, awaiting their employer's reaction. The firsthand report I received from one of them went something like this:

"All of a sudden, Carole's voice came over the loudspeaker,

reverberating against the tile floor and walls. It was plenty loud. She said, 'Aren't you a lousy looking sight sitting there with your balls hanging out?'

"There was a helluva scramble in the john. The door to the cubicle slammed open and Myron came out, pulling up his pants and looking wild-eyed about the room. He thought she was in there and it scared the hell out of him."

It is doubtful this changed Mr. Selznick's morning routine, but Carole and a handful of others got a well-deserved laugh out of the escapade.

On the "Silver Theater" broadcasts, following the musical curtain which closed the final act, host Conrad Nagel would often introduce the star of the program who then stepped out of character to endorse the sponsor's product. On one of the broadcasts on which Carole Lombard appeared, it was her after-the-show chore to speak on behalf of a new International Silverware pattern which had been trademarked *Interlude*. The copy which she was supposed to read began approximately thus:

International Silver Company's brilliant new pattern, Interlude, is one that may well be the June Bride's proudest possession. The bride who has Interlude on her dining room table will want Interlude in every room of the house.

Some wag conceived the idea that this would be the ideal time to turn tables and pull a gag on Carole. The plot went forward:

In the read-through she had already rehearsed the commercial, but when it came time to go on mike for balance and timing, she was told there'd be a change and—though the copy hadn't yet been delivered—it would be handed to her in time to be included in the proper spot at the end of the rehearsal. At the very last moment, during Nagel's introduction of Carole, one of our staff hurried into the studio, slipped the revised page into her script, giving her no time in which to so much as glance at it. Then, as Nagel ended his introduction with, ". . . and now, Miss Carole Lombard," she stepped to the mike and began to read:

The bride who has Intercourse on her dining room table will want Intercourse in every room in the house. . . .

Carole read that far without fully realizing what she had been saying, then, unconsciously executing a beautiful "double take", blurted out "Intercourse! What in—?"

Breaking off, she glanced up at the control booth to see all of us doubled over with laughter. She paused for an instant, a grin spread over her face and she exclaimed, "Why, you dirty—" and broke into laughter before she could complete the sentence. Then, as the full import of the situation struck her, she added, "Ohhh, no! . . . You bastards recorded that, didn't you?!"

We had recorded it. And whoever swiped that recording from my office undoubtedly still cherishes a "collector's item".

Although Carole and I had developed an excellent rapport during her several "Silver Theater" appearances, I was nevertheless astonished when one day she told me she'd like me to direct her next picture. Myron Selznick had informed her that Universal Pictures had requested her services as star of a comedy they were planning to produce. Carole had read the script which had been sent to her, liked it, and so informed the studio. But she made a stipulation which was completely unexpected. "I told Universal," she said, "that I would do the picture only if I could name my own director." Carole smiled at me, adding, "And that's you."

I protested that I had never directed a motion picture. "You can do it," she insisted. "If a stage director can direct a movie, so can a radio director. And you've got the same wacky feel for comedy that I have."

That was in late 1941. On December 7th the Japanese bombed Pearl Harbor. Shortly thereafter, Carole embarked upon a Defense Bond Drive. (On the steps of the State House in Indianapolis her exhortations resulted in the sale of over two million dollars worth of the bonds). Just before departing, she called to tell me she'd made an appointment for the two of us on Monday, January 19th, with the producer at Universal. She'd be back on the weekend previous to that date and would call me on Monday to confirm the time. I was both flattered and eager, for such an assignment represented an opportunity as rare as it had been unexpected.

But on the morning of January 17th I was awakened with the news that her plane had crashed the previous night, killing

Prelude to tragedy: Carole Lombard participates in a World War II Defense Bond Drive. Seen with her are (l.) Eugene C. Pulliam, California State Chairman of the drive, and Will H. Hays, President of the Association of Motion Picture Producers.

all on board. My first reaction was one of shock. Then came disbelief, with which I said one of those foolish things people are apt to say at such times: "She *can't* be dead. I have a date with her on Monday."

The whole nation was stunned—Hollywood most of all. That Sunday, Carole was to have been a guest on the Jack Benny program. Upon hearing of her death, Jack canceled the broadcast and could think of nothing better to do than to pace the sidewalks of Beverly Hills fighting back the tears. "That 'show must go on' stuff is a lot of crap," Jack said bitterly. "Especially at a time like this."

Within weeks, Clark Gable, desolate in his grief and painfully aware his wife had met her death in the service of her country, enlisted in the United States Army Air Force.

4

Other Favorite
Characters

During the hiatus which followed the first thirteen weeks of "Silver Theater," I was producer of the "Phil Baker Show," which was temporarily originating in Hollywood during Baker's appearance before the cameras in *The Goldwyn Follies*. At that time, the cast of Phil's show included Ward Wilson ("Beetle," his offstage heckler), Harry McNaughton (Phil's "veddy-veddy" English butler), a rising young comedienne, Lucille Ball, tenor Al Garr, Oscar Bradley's orchestra, and announcer Tom Hanlon.

The producer whom I had succeeded went over the program details with me, concluding our session by handing me a list of telephone numbers of the cast members whom I was to call for rehearsals. Other than Phil, I had met none of them at that time, but introduced myself to each as I contacted them regarding rehearsal time. Nothing unusual happened until I placed my call to Lucille Ball. I dialed her number. Promptly, a feminine voice answered. "Miss Ball?" I asked.

"Who's calling?" came the reply.

"Mr. Taylor," I said, assuming she'd been told the name of the program's new director. (As it turned out, my assumption was wrong).

"One moment, please," said the voice on the phone, "I'll call her."

In a matter of seconds, Lucille came on the line. Before I

Comedian-accordionist Phil Baker, known to millions of radio listeners as "The Great American Trouper."

A former model and Broadway stage actress, Lucille Ball made her motion picture debut in "Roman Scandals" in 1933. In 1938, she was a "regular" on "The Phil Baker Show" while the radio series originated in Hollywood during Phil's film engagement in "The Goldwyn Follies."

had an opportunity to introduce myself, and without so much as first saying "Hello," Lucille greeted me with a line which certainly would have amused famous screen lover Robert Taylor: "For Chris'sake—not *Bob!*"

No wonder a whole nation adopted the phrase, "I Love Lucy!"

Before radio, Phil Baker was best known—especially to vaudeville audiences and devotees of musical comedy—as a comedian who played accordion. For seven years his stooge was Sid Silvers who, working from a box just above the stage, insulted and heckled him. (Beetle, played by Ward Wilson whose voice was heard over a loudspeaker, was Sid's radio counterpart). Although a good showman, Phil was a less-than-sensational accordionist, so had not expected to be approached by a prominent accordion manufacturer seeking an endorsement for his instruments. The honorarium, as I recall, consisted of a beautiful multivoiced accordion plus considerable visibility through printed advertising and promotion.

"Gee," said Phil modestly, "how come you selected me? There are a lot of better accordion players."

"I know," said the manufacturer's spokesman, with unconscious frankness, "but you're the only one who's working steadily."

Phil was becoming bald by the time I started to work with him, never appearing in public without his toupee, unless its absence was disguised with a beret. While working in the *Goldwyn Follies,* he entered the big sound stage preparatory to going before the camera, when he encountered the fastidious Adolph Menjou who was also appearing in the movie. Menjou took one look at the toupee atop Phil's head and exclaimed, "My God! Where did you get that piece?"

Then, before Phil could reply, Menjou added, "Wardrobe will take advantage of a newcomer every time. You go right back there and tell them to give you a decent hairpiece!"

"Phil turned beet red," Menjou told me in recounting the incident. "Good Lord—I didn't know it was his own toupee!"

In April, 1938, the "Phil Baker Show" returned to New York, its star's home base, and continued to originate there until the thirty-nine-week cycle ended in June. At rehearsal for the final program, Phil and I had a slight argument over the pro-

The debonair Adolphe Menjou, who once advised comedian Phil Baker that the Goldwyn Studio's wardrobe department had furnished him with a terrible toupee, unaware that the "scalp doilie" Phil was wearing was his own.

"Blondie" was popular not only as a comic strip in newspapers but enjoyed much success in movies and in radio. Here, Arthur Lake (Dagwood) clowns it up with one of his special sandwiches as Penny Singleton (Blondie) worries about his digestive processes.

priety of a joke in the script. I finally convinced Phil the gag should be deleted then, to smooth his ruffled feathers, I kidded, "Don't worry, Phil. After this week's show I won't be getting in your hair any more."

Grinning, Phil replied, "I'll mail it to you."

Though Phil was an excellent comedy performer, he was not known for quick repartee. But on one occasion he came up with one which might be considered a minor classic: Phil, whose real surname was Shapiro, was Jewish. Invited by friends to play on a certain Westchester County golf course, he was about to tee off when an assistant manager emerged from the clubhouse. Approaching Phil with considerable diffidence, he said, "Pardon me, Mr. Baker . . . This probably embarrasses me as much as it does you, but this is a restricted club, and I have to ask you to leave."

"But I'm a guest of one of your members," Phil politely protested.

"Nevertheless, sir, we can't permit you to play."

There was a pause during which, undoubtedly, Phil was making an effort to control his anger. Succeeding, he assumed a wistful air and calmly asked, "Couldn't I play just *nine* holes? My wife's a gentile."

~~~~~~~~~~~~~~~~~~~~

One delightful interlude during my years at Young & Rubicam was thirteen weeks spent in New York producing and directing the Jack Benny 1941 summer replacement program, "Reg'lar Fellers." The series was based on the then popular newspaper comic strip of the same name, created by cartoonist Gene Byrnes.

Cartoonist Gene Byrnes, creator of the syndicated comic strip, "Reg'lar Fellers," sketches as he talks with the cast of the radio series based upon the newspaper feature. Seated next to him is Richard Monahan; standing (l. to r.) are Richard Van Patten, Eddie Phillips, and Ray Ives. The show was a summer replacement for the Jack Benny program.

Jack Benny looks over actress Ann Sheridan's shoulder as they inspect sound-effects equipment used on Jack's show.

*Jerry Devine, creator/director of the radio series, "This is Your F.B.I.,"
inspects one of the many confiscated weapons in the I. D. room of the
F.B.I. in Washington, D. C. Jerry wrote the "Reg'lar Feller" scripts.*

The radio series, "This is Your F.B.I.," recreated the motion picture, "The House on 92nd Street" and starred members of the original cast: (l. to r.) Jerry Devine (director), Reed Hadley, William Eythe, Signe Hasso and Lloyd Nolan.

The cast included several excellent child actors, among them Ray Ives, Jr., Eddie Phillips (discovered in a Harlem dramatic school), Patsy O'Shea, Dickie Monohan, Skippy Homeier, and Dick Van Patten.

(Directing an all-juvenile cast can be very nourishing to a director's ego: he has complete authority, the actors never argue, and even have to request his permission to indulge in the luxury of taking time out to go to the bathroom).

All the youngsters have had successful careers; many may remember that Skip Homeier later played important movie roles. Still later, Richard Van Patten gave me startled pause when he showed up on my television screen in the role of a baldheaded TV station manager on the "Dick Van Dyke Show"; he was a regular in that series. Later, he starred in the TV series, "Eight is Enough." Richard Monahan did well in motion pictures for several years.

Harry Von Zell was the "Reg'lar Fellers" program announc-

For his radio series, "This is Your F.B.I.," author/director Jerry Devine often went on location to secure special sound effects. Jerry (l.) and sound engineer George Otte are squatting behind the portable recording equipment as they capture authentic baseball sounds. Behind them stands Billy Meyer; at bat is Ralph Kiner.

er. My assistant director was a brilliant young fellow by the name of Robert E. Lee who later gained fame as the author (in collaboration with Jerome Lawrence) of such notable plays as *Inherit the Wind* and *Auntie Mame.* The author of the radio scripts for "Reg'lar Fellers" was Jerry Devine, a prolific writer best known to radio fans for his long running series, "Mr. District Attorney" and "This is Your F. B. I."

Jerry, always quick with repartee, made one of his many quotable remarks as we sat watching a *Fitzpatrick Traveltalk* in the Radio City Newsreel Theater where we were accustomed to kill time between the early and late broadcasts of "Reg'lar Fellers":

The subject of the *Traveltalk* was New Orleans, with colorful shots of men and women in *ante bellum* costumes posing on wrought-iron enclosed balconies and wandering beneath moss draped trees in City Park. One sequence in the film depicted the loggia of famed Arnaud's restaurant, reputed to be on the site where Napoleon Brandy was first dispensed in America. Before serving the exotic liquid, a waiter—his crooked elbow supporting a demijohn—approached and stood before a pedestal, atop which was a bust of Napoleon. Grasping the thong dangling from the clapper of a suspended bell, he clanged it loudly, clicked his heels, bowed stiffly, then turned to serve the beverage at a nearby table.

Immediately, Jerry—referring to a well-known New York restaurant which catered to show business people and specialized in kosher food—announced, "They do the same thing at Lindy's with herring and a statue of Bismarck." The theater audience broke into applause.

━━━━━━━━━━━━━━

While I was never producer of Eddie Cantor's programs, I did have a rather lengthy association with Eddie in a supervisory capacity. I acted as a buffer between the show's producer, David Elton, and Cantor, policing the scripts in matters of taste and otherwise interpreting sponsor and agency policies. Some of my experiences were, to say the least, interesting.

Eddie's sponsor at the time was the Bristol-Myers Co., manufacturers of Ipana toothpaste and the laxative, Sal Hepatica.

Somewhere along the line—long before I became associated with the show—there had developed a policy of teletyping from Hollywood to New York the entire script of the one hour program for sponsor approval. It was an awkward procedure as well as an expensive one, for it took a considerable length of time to transmit and the script used thirty-five or forty feet of teletype paper. The procedure was further complicated by someone's bright idea of having the teletype transcribed into script form at the New York end of the line and copies sent to sponsor and agency personnel. Thus gathered about a conference table in the sponsor's office were vice-presidents and other executives assuming the roles of the Cantor show's cast. There they would read aloud the dialogue that would ultimately be performed by professionals. Consequently, each week's script was judged on the basis of a performance by amateurs who were unaware of nuances and who hadn't the slightest notion of how to handle a straight line, a throw-away line or a punch line and probably thought "timing" was something applicable only to boiling an egg. As a result, a perfectly good comedy line or sequence would often be criticized as "unfunny," "makes no sense," or "it doesn't come off."

The teletyped critiques emanating from New York would, therefore, cause considerable frustration and cursing at the Hollywood end by producer, supervisor, and Cantor. In one particular instance, Cantor, who was noted for his volatile temper, concluded his anti-agency/sponsor tirade with, "Goddamit—they're anti-Semitic!"

Attempting to placate the irate star, producer Dave Elton explained, "But, Eddie—you can't say that. Fred Wile, who sent the teletype, is Jewish."

"The very worst kind!" shouted Cantor.

I was present at one rehearsal when Wendell Williams, NBC's Hollywood Continuity Editor, objected to an Eleanor Roosevelt gag in the script. I agreed with him it was in questionable taste and should be deleted. Eddie's banjo eyes bulged in protest:

"Just to show you what smart asses you guys are, I'll have you know I made a long distance call to Stephen Early, and he said the joke was okay." (Early was President Roosevelt's spokesman in press matters).

We proceeded with the rehearsal but, meanwhile, Williams —suspecting Cantor might have been less than truthful regarding the approval he claimed to have received from Washington— placed a person-to-person call to Early. Shortly thereafter the continuity editor came to the studio and informed Elton and me that Roosevelt's spokesman had denied speaking with Cantor. Early, after hearing the joke read by Williams, then requested it not be aired over NBC. However, in a diplomatic attempt to permit Cantor to save face, Williams decided to acknowledge that Eddie *had* made the call:

"I spoke with Mr. Early," the continuity editor told Cantor, "and he told me that when he spoke with you, you must have misunderstood. He says he asked you *not* to use that joke."

Eddie looked at us coldly for a moment, then snorted in disdain. "You're all a bunch of liars!" he exclaimed illogically. "I never called Mr. Early in the first place!"

Comedian Eddie Cantor (r.) scans a radio script with Walter Winchell, the syndicated columnist familiar to radio fans for his ebullient greeting, "Good evening, Mr. and Mrs. America—and all the ships at sea!" During a visit to Hollywood, Winchell appeared as a guest on "The Eddie Cantor Show."

Eddie finally consented to delete the joke, but somehow we got the impression that he was convinced he'd won the argument.

While Cantor may have been a difficult performer to handle, it must be said that he left behind a very worthy monument: the annual March of Dimes campaign. These drives raised funds which contributed mightily to medicine's ultimate victory over poliomyelitis. Cantor conceived the idea after a visit to Warm Springs, Georgia, where he had observed President Roosevelt and other polio victims (Eddie was particularly touched by the crippled children) undergoing therapy in the rejuvenating waters.

The late Fred Allen was a gold mine of anecdotes, many of them pertaining to his dislike of network and advertising agency executives—a dislike triggered by what he considered to be their unnecessary harassment of writers and performers, himself in particular.

One agency vice-president was referred to by Allen as "That ulcer with suspenders."

Of another he remarked, "He arrives at his office at nine in the morning, finds a molehill on his desk, and has until five in the afternoon to make a mountain out of it."

But his classic blast at those who breathe the rarefied air of the upper echelons was a good-natured one in the form of a letter addressed to John F. Royal, then Vice-President in Charge of Programs for the National Broadcasting Company. As a humorous sequence on one of Allen's programs, Fred interviewed a Captain Knight, owner of an eagle which had been trained in falconry. The broadcast originated in NBC's huge 8-H studio in Radio City, New York. The bird, secured at first to its owner's wrist, was eventually loosed to fly above the audience and return.

In radio's early days—before taping made it possible for a program to be easily recorded for release at a later hour—the Allen program's first broadcast of the evening originated in New York at 9:00 P.M. for the eastern/midwestern leg of the network; it was again performed "live" at midnight for a 9:00 P.M. (Pacific Time) airing on NBC's Pacific Coast network. Mr. Royal, who was the personification of dignity and decorum,

One of radio's most famous comedy teams: Fred Allen and his wife, Portland Hoffa.

heard the early broadcast and experienced misgivings when Allen described the eagle's flight about the studio. Fearing an "accident" might be bad public relations or even result in lawsuits claiming indignities or ruined clothing, he issued an edict that the eagle must not be permitted to fly during the repeat broadcast at midnight. Allen, always a nonconformist, resented Royal's highhandedness although he did abide by the ruling. Ironically, on the repeat show the eagle—fortunately chained to his master's wrist—*did* proceed to empty his bowels, thereby producing what was undoubtedly the longest laugh ever heard over a radio network. This brought the wrath of Mr. Royal down upon Fred's head a second time. The comedian blithely retaliated with the aforementioned letter which is herewith presented just as Fred typed it in his famous lower-case style:

dear mr. royal . . .

am in receipt of your letter commenting on l'affaire eagle as they are calling it around the Young & Rubicam office.

i thought i had seen about everything in radio but the eagle had a trick up his feathered colon that was new to me. i thought, for a minute, I was back on the bill with lamont's cockatoos.

an acolyte from your quarters brought news to me, following the nine o'clock broadcast, that the eagle was to be grounded at the midnight show. it was quite obvious that mr. ramshaw, as the eagle is known around the falcon lounge of the audubon society rooms, resented your dictatorial order. when his cue came to fly, and he was still bound to captain knight's wrist, mr. ramshaw, deprived by nature of the organs essential in the voicing of audible complaint, called upon his bowels to wreak upon us his reaction to your martinet ban.

toscanini, your house man, has foisted some movements on studio audiences in 8-h, the bulova company has praised its movement over your network, but when radio city is being torn down to make way for another mcguinness restaurant, in years to come, the one movement that will be recalled by the older radio fans will be the eagle's movement on wednesday last. if you have never seen a ghost's beret you might have viewed one on mr. rockefeller's carpet during our sterling performance.

i know you await with trepidation the announcement that i am going to interview sabu with his elephant some week.

yours for a wet broom in 8-h on wednesday nights.

fred allen

George Burns of radio's popular "Burns and Allen Show" (later a hit on television) is one of the funniest men with whom I ever worked. Although George's radio shows were rarely tinged with off-color material, in his private moments he often enjoyed using the "shock technique" on his listeners. A four letter word at a cocktail party when it was least expected was good for a laugh from those who overheard George's remarks, but often left a dignified hostess completely devastated for several minutes. An example:

HOSTESS: (extending tray of goodies) Would you like an hors d'oeuvre, Mr. Burns?
GEORGE: Don't mind if I do.
HOSTESS: (pointing to one of the delicacies) This one is nice.
GEORGE: (all charm and smiles) No, thank you. If you don't mind, I'll have this one with the shit on it.
HOSTESS: (blushes and gasps)

The victims of this shock effect gag were usually unable to think of a retort. George got his laughs from the bystanders and was very happy. But he had one teeny weeny fault: he couldn't bear to have anyone "top" him—a trait not unfamiliar to comedians, and which surfaced at the Hollywood Brown Derby restaurant during a lunch time conference at which I was present. Chris, one of the Derby's most alert waiters, approached our table, pencil and order pad at the ready:

CHRIS: Good afternoon, gentlemen . . . What will it be today?

GEORGE: (removing the cigar from his mouth) I'll have a glass of shit with an egg in it.

CHRIS: (straight-faced and without pausing) How would you like your egg?

While the rest of us at the table went limp with laughter, George returned the cigar to his mouth, clamping it between his teeth. He remained tight-lipped during the interval in which Chris jotted down the orders the rest of us had given. George then placed his legitimate order and began discussing other matters.

That George Burns is a funny man is not only my opinion, but that of millions of other people. Jack Benny was particularly susceptible to George's comedic gifts. Sometimes when we'd be sitting around the advertising agency's conference room table working on the script for the Burns and Allen program, Jack Benny—whose show was produced by the same agency—could be heard approaching. George, grinning, would say, "Watch . . . When Jack comes in, I'll make him laugh."

A script-reading session prior to a rehearsal for "The Burns and Allen Show" (1941). (l. to r.) Paul Whiteman, George Burns, Gracie Allen, vocalist Jimmy Cash, and supporting cast.

The radio series, "Tommy Riggs and Betty Lou" was at one time a summer replacement for "The Burns and Allen Show." Seated (l. to r.) are the writers of "Tommy Riggs and Betty Lou," George Balzer, Sam Perrin and **Jack Douglas. Kibitzing on the card players are director Glenhall Taylor (l.) and star Tommy Riggs.**

A moment or so later, the conference room door would open. Jack would glance about the room and give his usual deadpan greeting: "Hi, fellas." There would be simultaneous acknowledgments from all except George. With exquisite timing, he would wait for a moment, then removing the cigar from his mouth, would flick the ashes from it saying in a flat voice, "Hello Jack." It never failed; Jack would invariably break into a laugh as though someone had just told him a brand new, hilarious joke.

Speaking of Benny, old time radio fans will remember the charming, cricket-voiced black girl, Butterfly McQueen, who portrayed Jack's maid. Like her male counterpart in the fictional Benny household, Rochester (played by Eddie Anderson), she was a much loved favorite of the radio public and her disappearance from Benny's show was certainly radio's loss. According to Jack himself, it came about thusly:

Tommy Riggs welcomes cowboy star Roy Rogers. Roy's horse, Trigger, made his first radio guest appearance on the "Tommy Riggs and Betty Lou" show, whinnying and pawing his hooves on cue. For the studio stunt, the horse was shod with rubber horseshoes.

Butterfly McQueen, as she appeared in the motion picture, "Gone with the Wind." The lovable actress was a long-time favorite on "The Jack Benny Show".

A well-meaning representative of the National Association for the Advancement of Colored People had made continuing calls upon Butterfly, arguing that she should not demean herself by playing a housemaid. (Such approaches had also been made to Eddie Anderson who for years had portrayed Jack's butler. But Eddie, being of a more pragmatic mind, considered his $1,750 per week salary and remained uninfluenced). The NAACP apparently prevailed upon Butterfly to leave the show. Shortly before her departure became a *fait accompli*, Jack said to a group of us:

"Good grief! I'm paying Butterfly 750 dollars a week. Where else can she get that kind of money? Besides, everybody loves her. I don't think she's demeaning herself."

Three of radio's most famous personalities: Jack Benny, Rochester (Eddie Anderson), and the funniest automobile ever heard by human ears—Jack's temperamental Maxwell.

Jam (ham?) Session: Jack Benny fiddles while Harpo Marx plucks.

We agreed, expressing hope that Jack could somehow convince her to remain on the show. After all, Butterfly and Mary Livingston were the only feminine voices regularly heard on the series. Jack was thoughtful for a long moment. "Gee!" he finally said in that famous manner of his, "What does she want to do—play Mary's sister?"

Jack waited a bit, then grinning, added, "No. She wouldn't want to do *that*. Mary's Jewish."

~~~~~~~~~~~~~

"Red Ryder", based upon the nationally syndicated comic strip of the same name and starring Reed Hadley in the title role, was heard on NBC's Pacific Coast Network five afternoons a week. In this Western series, Ryder's faithful companion, the Indian boy "Little Beaver", was portrayed by a talented child actor, Tommy Cook.

Like most child actors, Tommy had a very protective mother. While she didn't interfere during rehearsals, she otherwise hovered over him. During the broadcasts she kept a watchful eye on him through the window of the sponsor's booth while listening to the performance over the loudspeakers. Aware of this constant vigil, Jerry Hausner, an accomplished actor who was also a talented prankster, enlisted the cooperation of writer-producer Paul Franklin, the show's announcer, and other members of the cast. He then contrived his mischief.

At the end of each broadcast just before giving the network cue, the announcer's procedure was to plug the next day's program. This was also done during the dress rehearsal. On this particular day, Hausner wrote the brief announcement concerning the coming program, and handed it to the announcer who at the end of the "dress" dramatically urged "Tune in tomorrow at this same time, when death comes to Little Beaver!"

Tommy's mouth flew open. The studio door flew open. Mrs. Cook flew in. Her reaction was precisely that which Hausner had anticipated. After a year or more of continuing performances with a very lucrative income, her Tommy was being written out of the show! How could they do such a thing?! Only after the cast had finally given in to laughter and the joke explained to

Reed Hadley appeared in many motion pictures and his splendid voice narrated many documentary films, but he was best known to radio listeners as "Red Ryder"—the hero of the series based upon cowboy-artist Fred Harmon's famous syndicated cartoon strip.

Members of the "Red Ryder" radio series celebrate an anniversary of the program. Standing in the rear are (l. to r.) engineer Carl Lorenz, announcer Carleton KaDell, Tommy Cook (Little Beaver, Ryder's Indian-boy companion), and supporting players Horace Murphy and Al Von Antwerp. Cutting the cake is Janet Waldo who also starred as Corliss Archer in the series of that title. Seated (l. to r.) are Paul Franklin, director/writer, and Art Rush, the agent who packaged the show.

her did Mrs. Cook recover from the shock. The role of Little Beaver remained permanent, of course, and Tommy continued to perform it with his accustomed skill. However, none of the "Red Ryder" stock company's cast was certain thereafter that Mrs. Cook was ever the same.

Out of the many pranks pulled at rehearsals, another stands out in my memory. A large San Francisco baking company sponsored a Pacific Coast Columbia Network series, "The Phantom Pilot." As the title might suggest, it was aimed at a juvenile audience. The Phantom Pilot might be likened to a Lone Ranger with wings (the wings being those of his speedy super plane, "Skyball"), rescuing the good people from the bad guys and seeing that justice was done. The program opening was actually quite effective. The announcer stood back from the microphone and in a dramatic stentorian voice projected, "The Phantom Pilot rides in Skyball!" Instantly there followed the revved-up snarl of a streaking plane takeoff. Then, as the sound-effect plane gained altitude and faded into the far distance, the announcer spoke again telling of the excitement to follow.

Between the dress rehearsal and air time while producer Carroll O'Meara was occupied elsewhere, the sound effects man and the announcer got their heads together and framed him. The studio and control booth clocks were set ten minutes ahead. Air time arrived sooner than O'Meara anticipated. Glancing at his watch and concluding that it must be slow, he hurriedly called the cast into the studio. Everyone was soon in mike position, ready to go. The minute hand and second hand synchronized "straight-up". From the control booth, O'Meara cued the announcer with a rapier-like thrust of his forefinger. "The Phantom Pilot rides in Skyball!" the announcer shouted. O'Meara cued the sound-effects man. The plane snarled its takeoff and was climbing into the wild blue yonder when the sound-effects man cranked up the recorded sound of a tremendous crash of tearing, buckling metal.

"Son of a bitch!" cried the announcer. "He didn't make it!"

O'Meara froze. His face went ashen. Despite the loud guffaws in the studio, it must have been a full minute before he recovered and the color returned to his face. The clocks were set back to the proper time and the victim joined in the laughter, albeit not so uproariously as the others. It was undoubtedly the worst moment of his broadcasting career. Later, during a script conference which involved actor Cary Grant, we played the recording of the bizarre performance.

"Good God!" exclaimed the suave Grant. "That was a terrible thing to do. The poor bastard might have died of a heart attack!"

~~~~~~~~~~~~~~~~

One of my most pleasant assignments in radio was as producer of the "Burns and Allen Show". In addition to the many laughs triggered by George, a close friendship which was to last until his passing developed between this writer and bandleader Paul Whiteman, whose music was a feature of the broadcasts. Paul's quick wit and unique gifts of hyperbole and simile were

Orchestra leader Paul Whiteman as he appeared on "The Burns and Allen Show" radio series. Paul not only conducted the orchestra but performed in comedy sketches with George and Gracie. The phrase, "with a no. 1 Crossley" refers to a now defunct audience rating service.

exceeded only by his warmth and generosity. A whole book could be written about the man known as the "King of Jazz," but in this account there is space enough for only a few anecdotes:

I recall one rehearsal during which the brass section consistently ignored his instructions to play softly. At length, his patience worn, he stormed, "If you guys don't stop making like Jericho with the studio walls, I'm gonna stuff grapefruit in those lousy horns!"

On another occasion, he had repeatedly told the members of the violin section that their instruments needed tuning. Finally, annoyed by the persistent out of tune playing, he pressed the button of the control booth talkback and snapped, "Goddamit, you fiddlers are *still* out of tune. Whadda I have to do—come out there and paint *frets* on them goddam gourds?"

In the band on the Burns and Allen program was a Latin-American drummer by the name of Willie Rodriguez. Willie, no novice with a knife and fork, was considerably overweight—most of it conspicuous about his middle. Paul's nickname for

The "King of Jazz," Paul Whiteman, conducting the brass and woodwind sections of his orchestra.

The famous artist, John Decker, painted this Frans Hals-like, tongue-in-cheek portrait of Paul Whiteman, "King of Jazz."

the rotund musician, who also played kettledrums, was "The Blimp on the Timp".

In addition to Paul's staff man, Jimmy Mundy, two Hollywood arrangers regularly contributed scores to the band on the "Burns and Allen Show." One, Joe Glover, was always meticulously dressed in the latest fashions of the day. His attire usually consisted of a Norfolk jacket, well tailored slacks, neatly shined shoes and an Alpine-style hat with a huge beaver tail tucked into its ribbon at a jaunty angle. In addition, he had cultivated a bountiful mustache and luxuriant Van Dyke beard. When Joe first reported for work, Paul took one look at him and exclaimed, "Well, whaddaya know—Christ in Esquire!"

Many fans of old time radio may remember Ken Darby's great quartet "The King's Men," featured with the Paul Whiteman band in the 30's. (It was Whiteman, "The King of Jazz," who so christened the group). "The King's Men" later contributed to the success of many other top programs, including "The Fred Allen Show," "The Rudy Vallee Sealtest Program," and "Fibber McGee and Molly". Darby had sent Paul an audition recording; he had hired the group after hearing it, but had never seen them. When the boys finally arrived in New York and went to the NBC studios where Paul was rehearsing, they waited until the orchestra took a break. The maestro, laying aside his yard-long baton, looked inquiringly in their direction. According to Ken Darby, he could think of nothing better to say than, "Mr. Whiteman— here's the quartet you bought."

Paul sized up the four callow youths, then unsmiling but with eyes twinkling said, "There's not enough meat on the four of you to make a good sandwich." Then the big, portly maestro added, "Drop up to the Biltmore Roof tonight about seven thirty. Steaks will be on the house; you all need to be fattened up. And, incidentally—if you should pass a whale on your way, cut me off a piece of blubber."

Many radio shows did a lot of traveling to military camps during World War II. The personal appearances of favorite stars was of great help in building morale among the men in our armed services. One date we played with "The Burns and Allen Show" was at a naval base in Long Beach, California. We traveled by automobile (gas rationing coupons furnished by the

The King's Men quartet with Paul Whiteman in 1936. (l. to r.) Crafton (Bud) Linn, top tenor; Jon Dodson, 2nd tenor; Paul Whiteman; Radburn (Rad) Robinson, baritone; Ken Darby, bass/arranger/accompanist. The photo was taken on the occasion when Texas Governor James V. Alred inducted all five into the Texas Rangers.

military), going to the base in the morning and returning after the late broadcast that evening, during a blackout. In Paul's car was George Burns, his writer-brother, Willie, and announcer Bill Goodwin.

Aided only by the feeble pinhole beams of the tiny blackout lights on each front fender of his big Lincoln convertible, Paul was inching his way back to Hollywood when before he realized it, the car had left the road—its right wheels on the slope of an embankment. Paul braked the tilted car to a halt and leaned out the window in an attempt to see more clearly. As he peered into the blackness, he recalled that the Air Force medics had recommended the inclusion in the diet of the airmen a certain vegetable which would enhance night vision. Drawing his head back into the car, Paul turned and addressed the other occupants: "Anybody got a carrot?"

For nearly two years, it was my privilege to direct the radio series, "Adventures of Sherlock Holmes," starring Basil Rathbone and Nigel Bruce. It may come as a surprise to most readers that this turned out to be a madcap experience, for despite the elegant dignity of that splendid actor Basil Rathbone and the bumbling ingenuousness exuded by that other excellent performer, Nigel Bruce, the atmosphere was not only pleasant but sporadically hilarious. Both men were delightfully humorous and, as their English friends might call it, "frightfully unpredictable."

Parenthetically, it probably should be mentioned that Nigel Bruce's full name was William Nigel Bruce. As a youth, serving in the British military in World War I, he had dropped his first name because the despised Kaiser's given name was its German equivalent, and his son, the Crown Prince, was derisively referred to as "Willie"—a sobriquet any Britisher of the era would wish to avoid. However, Bruce's nickname, "Willie", eventually returned to favor and most of us called him that. Rathbone's nickname was "Bazz," although the mischievous Bruce often called him "Bazzy-Wazzy."

During a goodly portion of our broadcast season, Rathbone and Bruce were on "loan out" from their home studio, MGM, to Universal Pictures where they were engaged in making the *Sherlock Holmes* movies, in their day reputed to be the biggest money-making "B" pictures of all time. (They have also been lucrative in their many television showings). Through an arrangement with Universal Pictures, the two stars of the series were permitted to leave the motion picture lot at noon each Monday in order to accommodate the radio programs which were broadcast on Monday evenings over the Mutual Broadcasting System. (As with other shows previously mentioned, an early program originated in Hollywood for release in the East with the identical program repeated "live" three hours later for the West).

It was the custom of Rathbone and Bruce to stop at a supermarket on their way from Universal to the Mutual studios and purchase snacks which could be consumed during the first read-through of the radio script. (Their schedule was too tight to permit the luxury of restaurant dining). Almost invariably, they bought cartons of milk and a package of snails (those spiral shaped, frosted sweet rolls sometimes called "Danish") which

Basil Rathbone, costumed as Sherlock Holmes, joins Gracie Allen and George Burns in a satirical "whodunit" sketch. The mystery: "What on earth is George smoking?"

they called "sugar buns." As a result of their informal repasts, our studio became a sloppy shambles by the time rehearsals were concluded.

Left-over milk was often poured into ashtrays to extinguish cigarette stubs; remaining snails were disposed of in a fashion which never failed to send Rathbone and Bruce into gales of laughter. As I sat behind the huge window of the control room engrossed in following the script or making pencilled corrections, the two "dignified" Britishers would suddenly bombard the glass with their sugar buns. Though it happened week after week, I was invariably caught unaware and, as the sticky missiles came hurtling toward me, I would duck out of sheer reflex as they splattered against the glass. This delighted them no end and they never seemed to tire of it. As the broadcasts were performed before a studio audience, a clean-up crew had to go to work every Monday night before the audience could be admitted. Not the least of the job was removing the sugar frosting from the glass of the control room. In directing the *Sherlock Holmes* show, I was, as the British might say, "batting in a sticky wicket."

Both men were "naughty" in the British sense of the word— particularly Bruce, who loved to shock people if he thought it would produce a good laugh. I recall rehearsing one scene in which Holmes and Watson were stealthily entering a darkened room during their efforts to solve a mystery. It went something like this:

SOUND: *Footsteps Along Hallway . . . Establish, Then Halt.*
WATSON: (Normal Voice) What now, Holmes?
HOLMES: (Sotto Voce) Sssh! . . . Quiet, Watson!
WATSON: (Whispering) Oh . . . Sorry, old boy.
HOLMES: Careful, now.
SOUND: *Doorknob Turned . . . Pause . . . Door Slowly Creaks Open*
HOLMES: All clear, Watson. Light the gas jet.
WATSON: Righto.
SOUND: *Striking of Match . . . Puff of Flame as Gas Jet is Lit*

And the scene proceeded from there—at least it should have.

However, after the striking of the match, before the sound-effects man could produce the sound of the lighting gas, Willie took a deep breath and blew a loud, resounding raspberry that rattled the loudspeakers, following which he said in his best Dr. Watson mumble, "Ooops . . . Sorry, Holmes . . . Wrong gas!"

Among the many ways to stimulate the sale of defense bonds during World War II were special theatrical performances to which admission was gained solely through the purchase of bonds. "The Sherlock Holmes" show was one of several radio programs whose services were requested by the War Department. We gladly complied, giving sell-out performances in theaters in Santa Barbara and San Francisco. In the latter city, the show was broadcast from the stage of Loew's Warfield Theater, a large movie house.

A couple of incidents remain so clearly in my mind that I still laugh out loud whenever I think about them. The first, on this Santa Barbara-San Francisco junket, occurred in the Redwood Room of San Francisco's prestigious Clift Hotel. Our large party—Basil Rathbone and his wife, Ouida Bergere; Nigel Bruce; the English actress, Edna Best; writer Denis Green and his wife, Mary; supporting actors and others connected with the show— was seated around a large circular table close to the center of the room. Inevitably, it became the focal point for the eyes of the other diners.

Nothing out of the ordinary happened until the dessert course. The waiter, having taken the order, returned from the kitchen with desserts for everyone with the exception of Nigel Bruce, who had ordered a chocolate fudge sundae with crushed walnuts. After serving the rest of the party, the politely apologetic waiter approached Bruce, saying in a German accented voice which could be heard at several nearby tables, "I'm sorry, Mr. Bruce, but I have no nuts."

His bushy white eyebrows bobbing above his dancing eyes, the respected Dr. Watson pushed back his chair and stared aghast at the waiter then, with theatrical resonance, he exclaimed, "No nuts! . . . Ooooh, poor fellow!"

The laugh that went through the dining room would have been relished by Bob Hope.

But Willie Bruce was not one to rest on his laurels. On our

Nigel (Willie) Bruce, the beloved Dr. Watson of the long-running radio series, "The Adventures of Sherlock Holmes." This caricature was made by Alan Reave in 1942.

return trip to Hollywood, our party boarded the early morning "Daylight" streamliner and breakfasted in the dining car, afterward seating ourselves in the chairs reserved for us in the observation/parlor car. We were probably an hour out of San Francisco when Basil arose from his chair, tucked a folded newspaper under an arm and started to leave. Because our party was seated near the rear of the car, it was necessary for anyone going forward to pass between the two rows of passengers in their upholstered swivel chairs.

Basil, with his usual elegance, had proceeded about half way along the aisle when Willie, his eyes narrowing mischievously, called out in a loud voice to the Rathbone's six year old daughter: "Cynthia, darling—where's Daddy going?"

We didn't know what to expect, but obviously Bruce did, for little Cynthia—in a clear, piping soprano for all to hear—answered, "Daddy's going to do after breakfast plop plops!"

Despite the laughter, Rathbone never batted an eye. Dignified as ever, he continued on his way to the men's room. The back of his neck, however, was somewhat red.

Finally, in our ribald ramblings-on about Nigel Bruce, we come to what I consider to be the jewel in his Rabelasian crown: Entertaining the troops at sprawling Camp Roberts, a few miles north of Paso Robles, California, "The Adventures of Sherlock Holmes" was broadcast from the stage of the installation's huge auditorium. Between the early and repeat shows, our troupe were guests at cocktails and dinner in the officers' club. As might be expected—because of the attraction of our important stars, the C.O. and many others of the camp's "top brass" were in attendance, as were a visiting general and other officers from nearby military posts. Several were accompanied by their wives.

We were in the center of a privileged military group standing near the bar in the officers' club having cocktails when Bruce activated his bomb. With me was my recent bride to whom both Rathbone and Bruce had taken a liking. In the midst of the conversation Willie, who had been observing the two of us, called attention to the fact that we were newlyweds. The strangers about us reacted with the usual congratulations and pleasantries. Then, having gotten their attention, he asked my wife, "Barbara

—you're such a lovely girl, what do you see in this fella? He has such a weak chin."

We merely smiled indulgently, but Bruce was persistent. "What *do* you see in him, dear girl?" he again asked.

Barbara gave him a forthright answer. "I love him."

All eyes were now upon the two of us. "*Love* him!" Willie exclaimed in mock astonishment, then added, "Tell me—do you kiss his naughties?"

The reaction to the remark was indeed akin to the reaction to a bomb explosion: the group disintegrated, scattering in all directions. Even Basil, who over the years had become well accustomed to his partner's ribaldry, turned a deep scarlet. All that the usually quick witted Rathbone could utter was a shocked, "Willll-ie!"

The cocktail party was over; we were informed that dinner was being served.

It is difficult to reconcile *that* Nigel Bruce with the pixie who called his wife "Mum Bear," referred to himself as "Papa Bear," and whose Malibu Beach house was identified with a neatly lettered sign which read, "The Lair." Perhaps Tom McKnight, who had directed "The Adventures of Sherlock Holmes" a few years prior to my taking over was right when he stated, "Willie Bruce is England's answer to Bunker Hill."

5

Onward and Upward?____

In February, 1946, I was made a vice-president of Young & Rubicam. As such, I continued to manage the firm's Hollywood office and to supervise its radio activities on the Pacific Coast. Shortly thereafter, during a business lunch with Groucho Marx and Walter Bunker, who had succeeded me as producer of the "Dinah Shore's Open House" radio series, Walter said to the mustachioed comic, "Groucho, did you hear that Glen has just been made a vice-president?"

Groucho, then appearing regularly on Dinah's program, flicked the ashes from his cigar, jiggled his eyebrows, and looked at me over the rims of his glasses. "You better be careful," he admonished. "You could become the Calvin Coolidge of advertising agencies."

Taking Groucho's warning to heart, I resigned the Young & Rubicam vice-presidency in August, to become Manager of the Hollywood Office of N. W. Ayer & Son, Inc., another top ranking advertising agency. The most intriguing facet of the offer made to me by Ayer was the granting of permission to direct "outside" radio shows on a freelance basis. By October, I was directing my first non-Ayer show, "The Fabulous Dr. Tweedy," a Foote, Cone & Belding Agency production for Pall Mall Cigarettes starring Frank Morgan in the role of a zany college president. Frank was a delightfully amusing man—one of those happy people who function most perfectly with a nip or two beneath the belt. (As a matter of fact, the only time I ever heard Frank muff a line of dialogue during a broadcast was on

Dinah Shore boasts a long radio career: vocalist with Ben Bernie's orchestra, "The Lower Basin Street Chamber Music Society" and "The Eddie Cantor Show," she also hosted her own radio series, "Dinah Shore's Open House" back in the 1940's.

During a "Command Performance" rehearsal break, the Armed Forces Radio Service (AFRS) photographer caught (l. to r.) Groucho Marx (complete with leer), vocalist Georgia Gibbs, actor Frank Morgan and Bill Morrow who, for many years, teamed with Eddie Beloin as a writer for Jack Benny.

one occasion when the dress rehearsal ran late and he'd had no time in which to make his usual trip to the Key Club—an oasis across Vine Street from the NBC Hollywood studios).

As Frank's fans well remember, he excelled whether playing serious drama or lighthearted comedy, though he was superb in the latter. His brother Ralph was also an excellent actor but seldom deviated from straight dramatic roles. A friend of mine once asked Frank how he had happened to gravitate toward comedy portrayals rather than specialize, as had Ralph, in the serious side of acting.

"Well," said Frank, "when I first worked as an actor, it was the fad for the juvenile in white pants, sweater, and tennis shoes to leap onto the stage, hold aloft a racquet, and ask, 'Tennis, anyone?' . . . Well, I took my juvenile rôles seriously enough but, when *I* leaped out onto the stage, I was so obviously flat-footed, I got a laugh every time. So I decided I might as well be funny on purpose."

Frank's friends loved to recount incidents having to do with his tippling. For example, there was the night that a fire broke out in the upper story of the Morgans' Beverly Hills home. Frank was sleeping soundly, aided by his several "nightcaps" when the alarm was sounded. He leaped from his bed and ran outdoors. By the time the firemen arrived, there was a sizeable audience present. Hoses were being dragged across the lawn by the firemen, police had arrived to keep order and hold back the too curious. The usual hysteria broke out among the members of the Morgan household. Frank's wife, Alma (so the story goes), fled the house in her best mink coat, carrying a jewel box and a cage with a frightened, chirping canary. Frank, despite his pre-slumber tippling, was the only member of the household who remained calm. He was handling the situation in a masterly fashion, directing the firemen as to the best place to put the ladder, instructing them on how to reach the room where the conflagration had broken out, and otherwise maintaining discipline amid chaos. Frank, however, was stark naked.

Then there was the time when his yacht had won the transpacific race from Los Angeles to Honolulu: Frank had been having such a happy time below deck, he didn't know he'd arrived in Honolulu Harbor and had won the race until his crew informed him.

The last time I saw Frank was shortly after he'd won that race. It was at a dinner party in a private dining room adjacent to the foyer of Chasen's, the celebrated Beverly Hills restaurant. Seated around a large, circular table, we were sipping our after-dinner coffee as Frank was escorted into the room by Dave Chasen. Following a brief exchange of happy greetings, Dave announced, "Frank has something he wants to show you."

Frank had our undivided attention. He gave forth that famous giggle of his, then said, "I bet I've got something nobody else in this room has."

We waited, anticipating he might extract something strange from a pocket—a funny prop, perhaps, or some other form of visual gag. Instead, Frank unbuckled his belt, unzipped his fly, and dropped his trousers to reveal a dazzling leopard skin jockstrap; its shiny black spots seeming to leap out from their wild yellow background.

Bob Hope studies Dorothy Lamour, star of "Sealtest Variety Theater," instead of the script. The author, Glenhall Taylor, who directed the series, is having a hard time being serious.

It was a nice way to remember a fun-loving friend. A few weeks later, Frank's laughter was no more.

～～～～～～～～～～～～

In June, 1947 the N. W. Ayer agency assigned me to direct a new series of half-hour weekly radio shows to help stimulate enlistments in the United States Army. The series, "Front and Center," starred Dorothy Lamour as mistress of ceremonies and featured Hollywood radio and screen guest stars, a well-known quartet, The Crew Chiefs, and Henry Russell's orchestra.

My first meeting with the "queen of the sarong"—as Dottie was known, albeit the garment she made famous was actually a "sari"—was not in a hurricane backed by the strains of "Moon of Manakoora" (although Dottie herself was a breath of fresh air), but in the Polo Lounge of the Beverly Hills Hotel. Present in addition to Dorothy Lamour and me were Clarence Menser, NBC's Vice-President in Charge of Programs; the network's Pacific Coast Musical Director, Henry Russell; and Hal Hackett, Vice-President of the Music Corporation of America (MCA), the giant talent agency representing Dottie. Warm and unpretentious, she made lasting friends of Hank Russell and me with her disarming remark, "I can't sing and I can't act. It's up to you guys to make me sound good."

Hank and I, of course, had no doubts about her abilities, but she had given us a vote of confidence seldom offered in a profession where modesty is a rare commodity. During our long association with her, she never spoke an unkind word nor gave the slightest indication of temperament. She was and is a "pro", which she had occasion to prove during one of radio's greatest debacles:

The U. S. Army Recruiting Service's sponsorship of "Front and Center" enjoyed a thirteen-week run which began on July 6, 1947. The following year, its format unchanged, the series was resumed under the aegis of National Dairies, Inc., and retitled, "Sealtest Variety Theater." It began a thirty-nine week run in September, 1948. On St. Patrick's day in 1949, the debacle would occur.

Glenn McCarthy, a former Texas oil wildcatter who had become a millionaire businessman, had just completed the con-

Veteran actor Walter Brennan (r.) was one of the stars of the motion picture, "The Green Promise" which debuted in conjunction with the Shamrock Hotel's grand opening in Houston, Texas. He is seen here with Fr. Patrick Peyton who conceived the "Family Theater" series for radio and, later, for television.

10-year-old Natalie Wood co-starred in "The Green Promise"—the film which premiered during the official opening of Houston's Shamrock Hotel on St. Patrick's Day in 1949. (Hotel owner Glenn McCarthy was the producer). With Natalie is Max Terr, music director of the "Family Theater" series.

struction in Houston of one of the most ostentatious hotel buildings in America—the Shamrock—and had decided to throw open its doors to the accompaniment of an inaugural celebration as lavish as the hotel itself. As part of the festivities, he would present the premiere of "The Green Promise" which represented his debut as a motion-picture producer. The film starred Walter Brennan, Marguerite Chapman, Robert Paige, and a talented ten-year-old, Natalie Wood. In addition, McCarthy had requested that the Dorothy Lamour program originate in the plush Emerald Room of the hotel on the opening day, March 17th.

To understand the enormity of the preparations for that opening day, one must know at least a little of what was entailed. In addition to over forty press representatives and photographers, musicians, talent agents, radio engineers, and innumerable non show business personalities, the guest list included these well-known radio and motion-picture names:

Edgar Bergen	Sonja Henie
Ward Bond	Hugh Herbert
Walter Brennan	Dorothy Lamour
Gale Storm	Stan Laurel
Bruce Cabot	Constance Moore
Leo Carillo	Chester Morris
MacDonald Carey	Wayne Morris
Joan Caulfield	J. Carroll Naish
Peggy Cummins	Pat O'Brien
Joan Davis	Dennis O'Keefe
Andy Devine	Robert Paige
Brian Donlevy	Robert Preston
Wallace Ford	Duncan Rinaldo
Ed Gardner	Buddy Rogers
Kathryn Grayson	Ginger Rogers
Virginia Gray	Robert Ryan
Alan Hale	Robert Stack
Van Heflin	Ruth Warrick

With spouses and friends, over 100 people were transported by pullman, nearly as many by plane. The train was a Santa Fe Super Chief: sixteen cars, including a diner serving the excellent food traditional with the crack trains of that era, and two lounge cars stocked with enough liquor to cause a rail washout if they had collapsed in a wreck. With over a hundred people aboard and all that free booze, it was the day before prohibition all over again: people were consuming alcohol as though it would never again be available. The most cogent comment on the mass imbibing was made by actor Pat O'Brien:

One of the press photographers, who had been popping flash bulbs throughout the train until it became too late to be served in the diner finally quit working and entered the lounge car. Placing his camera on the floor by the wall of the car, he was ordering a sandwich from the bartender as Pat—himself happily buzzed—came through the car. Seeing the cameraman's equipment on the floor, Pat looked at him and said, "You hadn't better leave that there. Somebody'll drink it."

The Shamrock Special was a real swingin' train (although, in those days, the adjective was limited to describing dancebands). A number of us were traveling with our wives; some of the other men were traveling with "friends" or "companions" of the opposite sex which caused gravel-voiced actor Andy Devine (a teetotaler, by the way) to make the funniest remark of the trip: "If all the douche bags on this train were inflated, we could *float* into Houston like the Graf Zeppelin."

The Shamrock Special didn't float into Houston, but its arrival caused as much excitement as though it had. All the way from the railway station to the hotel, the streets were lined with welcoming fans. One estimate gave the number as over 300,000 —at that time, over a third of the city's population. The local papers reported that more people had turned out to see the "bunch from Hollywood" than had turned out even for President Roosevelt. After we had driven about four miles in the chauffeured limousines, the Shamrock suddenly loomed up before us. Though not a tall building compared to the high-rise monsters of Manhattan, its eighteen stories soaring upward from the surrounding plain seemed twice that height.

The hotel was among the first big ones constructed in the post World War II period and therefore among the most modern of its day. It boasted a 1,000 car garage, the "biggest bath towels **in the world**," a refrigerated garbage room, a 165 foot swimming pool with seven racing lanes ("Duffy Tavern's" Ed "Archie" Gardner claimed he saw whitecaps on it), a 100,000 pounds per

One of America's most beloved character actors. Andy Devine's gravel-voiced greeting, "Hi ya, Buck?" was first heard on Jack Benny's radio show in 1937. He was also featured in a radio series starring Roy Rogers, Dale Evans, and the Western singers, "Sons of the Pioneers."

week laundry room, noiseless elevators, a lobby the size of a basketball court, and nine dining rooms—including the Emerald Room from which our broadcast would originate. The Emerald Room's capacity was 1,000 diners or 1,500 dancers. *Life* magazine described it as being decorated in "international modern . . . dripping with murals and indirect lighting." (Frank Lloyd Wright, the famous architect who was a guest on opening day, described the edifice as a "tragic imitation of Rockefeller Center," adding that there should be a sign in front of it, its letters in electric lights spelling out W-H-Y?).

When we arrived on Wednesday, the day before the official ribbon snipping, pandemonium was already in command. Everyone in the milling crowd seemed to be an autograph hunter, including waiters who should have been serving food. Room Service was swamped, many people waiting until past midnight before they were able to get dinner. With all those guests arriving almost simultaneously, Valet Service was frustratingly confused. Chester Morris was over an hour late for dinner when a harassed valet abruptly quit and left the actor's tuxedo trousers, along with a huge pile of other guests' garments, on the hallway floor. And things were not about to get better.

When the arrangements for the broadcast to originate from the Shamrock were made, the hotel's representative had agreed that once our transmission lines were installed and our microphones set up, they would not be used for any purpose other than that of broadcasting "Sealtest Variety Theater." However, someone got the bright idea that celebrity interviews could be piped from the hotel to a local radio station. The result was an error that channeled our lines through the hotel's public address system, thereby causing the voices of actors, the show's music and sound effects to be broadcast minus both "highs" and "lows." Hank Russell's fine orchestra sounded like a performance on a 1920 acoustical recording emanating from a 1920 hand-cranked, portable phonograph; the actors sounded as though they had clothespins on their noses. To compound the difficulties, the Shamrock had oversold the Emerald Room's seating: 2,000 people tried to crowd into 1,000 seats! In addition, rather than not permitting the guests to be seated until just before broadcast time, the Emerald Room's doors were thrown open to the public

Actor Van Heflin as he appeared about the time he performed as guest on Dorothy Lamour's program, "Sealtest Variety Theater" at Houston's Shamrock Hotel in 1949.

early, resulting in a milling, shouting, cocktail-stimulated crowd which rendered normal conversation virtually impossible.

When we hit the air, Dorothy Lamour and Van Heflin were unable to hear each other's dialogue. Because the temporary control booth which had been installed was completely beyond their line of vision, I was forced to squat on the stage in front of them, finger-cueing first one then the other for each speech to be delivered. Raoul Murphy, the competent NBC engineer seated at the control panel, was twirling knob after knob in an effort to achieve some semblance of proper balance. His attempts were futile. Karel Pearson, the NBC contact producer who had remained in the control booth with Murphy, picked up the frantically ringing telephone's receiver. NBC Chicago was calling to inform us what we already knew: "The quality is lousy!" (The telephone broadcast lines were routed from Houston to Chicago from where, in turn, the program was relayed east and west). "This is the NBC producer," Karel shouted over and over trying to make himself heard above the tumult and distorted sound. Then it happened:

Raoul Murphy shook his head in helplessness, remarking half to himself as though thinking out loud, "They're fucking it up!" Almost unbelievably, his low-spoken words were picked up on the telephone some five feet behind him during Pearson's frenetic efforts to communicate with Chicago. To make matters worse, the communications line had somehow gotten crossed with the broadcast line, and the engineer's comment was heard from coast to coast. Moments later we were cut off the air and local stations all across the country began spinning phonograph records with which to replace the scuttled program. But in Houston, we continued to carry on, for it was not until later we were informed we'd been off the air. Meanwhile, Dorothy struggled valiantly against the odds of the tumult and cacaphony, first in the serious dramatic sketch with Van Heflin, then parrying the comic barbs of "Duffy Tavern's" "Archie." Finally, the program ended, she fled the Emerald Room to surrender to the tears she had bravely been holding back. I settled for a couple of double Scotches.

And still the elbow shoving went on among the guests who had paid forty-two dollars a plate to attend what was to have been a gala dinner event. "It was like trying to eat dinner in

Ed Gardner (center)—"Archie" of the radio series, "Duffy's Tavern"—is enjoying his guest stars, Frank Sinatra and Alice Faye. They are autographing Archie's bartender's apron, as did nearly all of his guest stars.

the Notre Dame backfield," commented movie columnist Erskine
Johnson. Ed Gardner accidentally poured a cup of coffee on Mrs.
Chester Morris' lovely blonde head. More guests pushed into
the already crowded room. The doors were closed in an attempt
to control the situation, but the crowd forced them open again.
One waiter, when asked for a cup of coffee, said, "Sorry. I
don't work here. I work four blocks down the street. I got caught
in the crowd." "I don't give a damn about your broadcast!"
one guest was heard to shout. "I paid for my seat and I want
in!"

Next day, the *Houston Press* summed it up in a huge, bold
lettered headline:

LAMOUR LOSES "BATTLE OF BEDLAM"

One might anticipate that we had sponsor difficulties after such
an expensive debacle (as I recall, our cost per program was
about $15,000, exclusive of network time costs—low by TV
standards, but definitely not chicken feed)—but no trouble
developed. The reason? Our newspaper clipping service revealed
that, as a result of the Shamrock "donnybrook", the program
received press coverage in every city of the United States with a
population of 11,000 or over, plus a large spread in *Life* and
feature articles in nearly all other national news weeklies. That
sort of publicity couldn't have been bought; it made up not only
for the program cost, but for the 1,000 chocolate eclairs which
Sealtest had shipped but which couldn't be delivered to the tables
in the Emerald Room.

Glenn McCarthy's tab for this Babylonian bash was reputed
to be in the neighborhood of $425,000, an amount which seems
credible in view of some of the excesses in which the tycoon had
indulged. He had 1,000 shamrocks flown in from Ireland; $1,000
worth of orchids decorated the trees in the lobby (they were
stripped bare by the time dinner was served); the cost of char-
tering the Santa Fe's Super Chief for seven days was $14,000
per day; aboard it, sumptuous meals including 144 sirloin steaks
and 75 lamb chops were served. Tips for the train's waiters
totaled $3,500. The beverage bill for the train trip plus the
1,200 bottles of champagne served to his guests at the hotel cost
McCarthy another $41,000. However, it may be assumed he could
afford this little self-indulgence: according to *Life* magazine,

he owned "nine companies, including newspapers, radio and movies, and is said to have at least $100 million worth of oil underground."

Upon returning to Hollywood, I learned that our engineer, Raoul Murphy, was in danger of losing his job because of his indelicate remark which had been inadvertently broadcast to the nation. I intervened with Sid Strotz, then Vice-President in charge of NBC's Western Division. At first, he was adamant: "Raoul had no right to use that kind of language in a control room."

I explained in detail that Raoul's back was to the telephone, that he was nowhere near a microphone, and told of the fouled-up lines and the pandemonium in the Emerald Room. I concluded my plea with one final appeal to his reason: "With everything going to hell like that, what else *could* he say?"

Strotz was a good sport. He threw back his head and laughed. "I guess you're right," he conceded. "We won't fire him."

Among the several N. W. Ayer radio shows I supervised was the "Durante-Moore Show," starring unforgettable Jimmy with the king-size nose, and the young, ebullient Garry Moore. "The Schnoz," a product of Coney Island honky tonks, speakeasies, vaudeville, and starring roles in Broadway musicals, had worked in radio on and off since the early thirties. But it was not until veteran radio producer Phil Cohan teamed him with Garry that Jimmy became established as a *top* radio personality. The good-looking, sophisticated younger man turned out to be an ideal foil for the arm-flapping, dese-does-and-dem dynamo.

Those of us who had continuing contacts with Garry remember him for his quick wit and offbeat sense of humor. Typical of the latter was the "unemployed party" he hosted at his Brentwood home shortly after he had decided to leave the "Durante-Moore Show" and strike out on his own. Attending were a score of "unemployed" performers whose radio shows had been canceled or who were on summer layoffs. Among the well-fixed "displaced persons" were Bud Abbott and Lou Costello, Alan Young, Hoagy Carmichael, Benny Goodman and Joan Davis.

In the garden of the Moore home, a gold-fringed canopy had been stretched above an arrangement of gilded bentwood chairs

(l. to r.) Chet Brouwer, radio publicist, Dorothy Lamour, Jimmy Durante and Glenhall Taylor. The occasion was the introduction of handpainted neckties bearing Jimmy's likeness (A publicity stunt, of course).

for the comfort of advertising agency executives and sponsor representatives. The poor, out of work performers had to settle for plain, wooden, foldaway chairs. There were sparkling highball glasses for the libations of the affluent employed, but only beer cans for the highballs of the unemployed. (Garry had drained the contents of two cases of beer for the purpose). Indoors, above the long buffet table was stretched a cloth sign which read:

THIS WAY TO THE BREAD LINE

Also typical of Garry's humor was the unusual belt he designed as a birthday present for Mrs. Moore. During the post-war years of the forties certain metalware products were still extremely difficult to obtain. But Garry was determined his wife's gift should be unique. After purchasing tours of a dozen or more stores, he managed to accumulate enough copper rivets with which to cover most of the surface of a luxurious wide leather belt he

Producer/director Phil Cohan ("always in the middle," he claimed) of "The Durante-Moore Show," tries to moderate a discussion between his two stars, Garry Moore (l.) and Jimmy Durante, while dining at the Hollywood Brown Derby restaurant.

had bought. These he arranged so that the belt fairly glistened with the bright metal. At a glance, it appeared to be merely a lavishly studded belt. However, on closer inspection, one became aware the rivets were arranged as letters—extremely closely spaced—but carrying a message:

MY NAME IS NELL MOORE I AM A MARRIED LADY
BUT THANK YOU JUST THE SAME.

Of course, the beautiful Nell had to pivot like a Powers model in order for an aggressive male to read it, but that served to heighten the joke.

One St. Valentine's Day, Garry combined his humor with sentiment when he hired a skywriter to emblazon against the blue yonder a message in fluffy, white vapor:

GARRY LOVES NELL

Unlike Garry's comedic touch, much of Jimmy's was not consciously created; rather, it "happened." His fans, regardless of the medium in which he may have entertained them, are familiar with his mangling of the English language. Often his malaprops were as good as, or even better than, the word for which he'd been groping. Certainly his exclamation, "It's a *cat*astrofe!" made the disaster sound much more cataclysmic than had the word "catastrophe" been pronounced correctly.

I like, too, a summing up remark made by Jimmy when he said, "Well, fellas, it all simmons down to this." Somehow the word "simmons" used in place of "simmers" conjures up an image of box springs or mattresses and, therefore, Jimmy's word seems to say, "this gets down to *bed*rock"—a firm foundation.

At a press function in the Beverly Hills Hotel, Jimmy Durante gazes in awe at an ice sculpture of himself.

One of the country's largest advertising agencies is Batten, Barton, Durstine and Osborn, for years known in the business as "B. B. D. & O." Even the firm's switchboard operators greet the caller with the initials instead of the cumbersome four name identification. During a script reading at Jimmy's home, someone in the Hollywood office of that agency telephoned Jimmy. Not wishing to disturb him, the script secretary took the message and slipped him a note requesting he call B. B. D. & O. as soon as he became free.

Actor/photographer Jerry Hausner captured this rare shot of three of the funniest men in show business during a "Command Performance" appearance, during World War II, for the Armed Forces Radio Service (AFRS). For the very few who may not recognize the trio, they are (l. to r.) Fred Allen, Jimmy Durante and Jack Benny.

During a break in the script session, Jimmy went to the telephone and returned the call. There was a pause as he awaited the pickup at the other end, then we heard him say, "Hello . . . Is dis d' railroad?"

Although Jimmy was actually aware of the agency, his quick mind had inadvertantly leaped back to his many years in the East where the "B. & O." (the Baltimore and Ohio Railroad) was as familiar to him as the Santa Fe was to westerners and transcontinental travelers.

One day Jimmy came into the studio both elated and touched over the fact that at an awards dinner the previous evening the B'Nai Brith had presented him with a "Golden Heart" plaque in recognition of his considerable efforts on behalf of Jewish charity activities. He was not only proud of the beautiful plaque —a golden heart mounted upon a handsome, grained wood escutcheon—but quite moved that he, a Catholic of Italian descent, had also been presented with a Judaic mezuzah.

A short while later, a uniformed NBC page entered the studio with a large, shoe box sized package which had been delivered to the building's artists' entrance for Jimmy. He had not been expecting a package, so as he began to unwrap it, speculated aloud, "Cheez! I wonder what's in it?"

Promptly, one of the writers replied, "Spare parts for the mezuzah."

For the barest instant, Jimmy was about to accept the statement but, suddenly realizing it was a spoof, fixed the culprit with an admonishing glare and said, "Dat just goes t' show ya—ya can't trust nobody."

For quite some time, Jimmy had signed off his radio programs with a phrase that eventually intrigued everyone who had heard it: "Goodnight, Mrs. Calabash, wherever you are."

Listeners wrote in to ask who Mrs. Calabash was. Radio columnists conjectured it might be an old flame of Jimmy's, or perhaps an old friend of whom he'd lost track. On those occasions when someone from the press interviewed Jimmy, an inquiry regarding Mrs. Calabash was almost certain to enter the interrogation. So many conflicting theories were advanced that eventually Jimmy himself became a victim of the fantasy. It wasn't long before he began to think she really existed, and found

Helen Traubel, Metropolitan Opera Star, is apparently aghast at Jimmy Durante's attempt to tackle an operatic aria. (Or is he singing "Nobody Knows the Traubel I've Seen?") Traubel guested on Jimmy's radio and television shows.

himself volunteering the information that she was an ardent fan whose many letters had intrigued him, and that he'd decided to acknowledge them by mentioning her name on the air. We suspected he'd come to actually believe it.

Throughout the years during which this mild controversy continued, the person most amused by the whole thing was the "Durante-Moore Show's" producer-director Phil Cohan, for he *knew* how the fictitious heroine came to be cast in the role.

It seems that Jimmy—at heart an incurable sentimentalist—was impressed by baritone John Charles Thomas's famous sign off on each of his weekly radio programs: "Good night, Mother."

"What a lovely thing for a guy to say," commented Jimmy to Phil. "I wonder if I could say something like that?"

When Phil reported Jimmy's idea to the show's writers, they agreed that Jimmy "might have something." So late one night, after the long script rewrite session which had followed the rehearsal, Phil and the writers began to "kick it around." Aware that whatever Jimmy's new sign-off might be, it should have a touch of humor, they began trying out names on one another, each man hoping his suggestion would be the one to earn laughing approval from his colleagues:

"Good night, Mrs. Abercrombie" . . . "Good night, Mrs. Balaban" . . . "Good night, Mrs. Fennerbessy" . . . "Good night, Mrs. Terwilliger" . . . "Good night, Mrs. dePeyster"; and so on and on until Phil, deep in concentration, struck a match, lit his calabash, puffed the tobacco into a glow, stared at the pipe in his hand and said, "Good night, Mrs. Calabash."

Intrigued with the improbable name which had suddenly come from "left field", Phil and the writers—mimicking Jimmy's style of delivering lines—repeated the line over and over until all were satisfied it was "pure Durante". Thus the famous catch phrase was born. Several shows later, it became, "Good night, Mrs. Calabash—*wherever you are.*"

As Jimmy continued to repeat the phrase week after week, interest in the mysterious Mrs. Calabash snowballed. So many letters arrived in the mail that it was well-nigh impossible to acknowledge each one personally, so reply postcards were printed. Phil Cohan recalls that the message above Jimmy's printed signature went something like this:

Thank you for your letter about Mrs. Calabash. I'd like to tell you about her, but there are some things a gentleman doesn't talk about.

As Phil put it: "Jimmy really wanted to believe in Mrs. Calabash. Her existence—mythical though it was—was very dear to him."

It might be added that in turn, it was this sort of ingenuousness that endeared Jimmy in the hearts of his audiences. If somewhere, there happens to be a *real* Mrs. Calabash who has been basking in the glory of her unearned fame, and if she should read this, I hope she'll forgive me—wherever she is.

6

It's Come

a Long Way, Baby!

It's a long way from 1884 to the middle of the twentieth century when coast-to-coast network television came into being. In 1884, a German inventor by the name of Paul Nipkow took out a patent on a mechanical image-scanning disk and transmitted pictures in his laboratory. In the 1920's, two American inventors, Vladimir Zworykin and Philo Farnsworth, created two gadgets which were immeasurably more practical—the iconoscope and the image dissector tube, respectively—and the development of television got a shot in the arm. But those of us who were looking forward to enjoying programs in our homes would have to wait awhile, for the beer can and the TV dinner hadn't yet been invented.

The first demonstration of home-reception television occurred in Schenectady, New York, on January 13, 1928, when RCA and General Electric installed three home sets to receive a telecast of sound and picture simultaneously—though on two different wave lengths. The picture was one and one-half inches square! The first *practical* demonstration, featuring the telecast of a half-hour variety program from two New Jersey experimental stations—W2XCD, Passaic, and W2XCR, Jersey City—took place on August 30, 1930. Three home sets in New York City received the program. One was in a Riverside Drive residence, another

156

in the Hearst Building at 8th Avenue and 52nd Street, and the third in a store at the corner of Broadway and 73rd Street.

The master of ceremonies was cartoonist Harry Hershfield, who introduced civic leaders and several well-known entertainers including George Jessel, humorist Arthur ("Bugs") Baer, Diana Seaby, and Benny Rubin. The program was broadcast over a distance of approximately six miles—the longest ever achieved at that time in this country.

So the era was launched, even though commercial television would have to wait until after World War II before coming to full fruition. The year 1946 closed with twelve stations in the United States operating commercially. By 1948, forty-six were on the air, with construction started on seventy-eight more and over 300 license applications filed with the Federal Communications Commission. (Today there are nearly 1,000 television stations in the United States).

Coast-to-coast network television was still in the future. Radio

Comedian George Jessel appeared on television as early as 1930. Looking over his shoulder as he gives George pointers on a script is veteran announcer Jimmy Wallington.

network programs had been carried across the country from station to station by equalized telephone lines capable of transmitting sounds of higher and lower frequencies than the unequalized lines suitable for mere person-to-person telephonic communications. But television required a broader band than radio, so even the equalized lines were incapable of transmitting a satisfactory picture.*

As early as 1936, the Bell System unveiled the first coaxial cable. It could carry hundreds of telephone conversations as well as numerous radio programs simultaneously. After television began its rise to popularity in the 1940's, coaxial cable was also used for video transmission over short distances. In 1946, TV coverage of the Army-Navy football game was transmitted to New York for broadcast, and regional transmissions of commercial programs were made over hookups between San Francisco, Los Angeles, and San Diego in the late 1940's and early 1950's.

Further refinements made greater distances possible through the use of repeaters. But even with repeaters, the television pictures transmitted via coaxial cable deteriorated as distance increased. Adding to the problem was the high cost of coaxial cable—about $65,000 per mile—which limited the growth of long haul routes.

Then, in 1947, the solution arrived with the introduction of microwave, a direct adaptation of radar technology developed during World War II. Utilizing radio waves in the ultra high-frequency band, microwave could be beamed point to point over long distances through a series of towers located about thirty miles apart. The transmission quality and economy of microwave became quickly apparent, and work on a coast-to-coast system was begun. (A 1973 cost study by A. T. & T. Long Lines shows the current cost of coaxial cable at $8.23 per circuit mile, compared to 3¢ per circuit mile for microwave!)

The early microwave systems had six channels, each carrying 480 voice circuits. Over the years, the capacity was increased until the newer system, utilizing a higher frequency, now has 1,800 circuits on 8 channels. Both the older and newer systems operate on the same towers without interfering with each other.

* Technical information supplied through the courtesy of David C. Hall, The Pacific Telephone and Telegraph Company.

Today, the nationwide microwave routes can handle several TV programs plus thousands of voice conversations simultaneously. There are several microwave routes, each with many "legs," which total 1,892 microwave stations in the United States. A direct television link between New York and Los Angeles requires 117 towers; more are added as additional coverage is required.

By August 1951, the Bell System had erected a coast-to-coast chain of radio relay towers. On the 17th of that month, the first long-distance transcontinental call was made by Wayne Coy, Chairman of the Federal Communication Commission, in New York. He spoke with Harold Hull of the California Public Utilities Commission in San Francisco. The inauguration of this vast relay system was indeed a communications milestone to be celebrated, and the Bell System decided to make a gala event of it by introducing the first . commercial broadcast use of the microwave on August 20th, (four weeks prior to the debut of transcontinental television) on the company's own program, "The Telephone Hour." The radio program, as usual, featured Don Voorhees' orchestra. The guest soloist was baritone Nelson Eddy. The musical portion of the program originated in the NBC studios in New York. For the West Coast origination point, symbolic Telegraph Hill, high above San Francisco Bay, was chosen.

I was assigned to produce the San Francisco segment of the program. Huddled in topcoats with the enveloping, late afternoon fog drifting through the arches on the crest of the tall, fluted Coit Memorial Tower on Telegraph Hill, the three of us shivered about the microphone which had been installed there for our use: Sam Dickson, NBC producer and noted San Francisco historian; Harry Bright, the San Francisco Public Relations Vice President of The Pacific Telephone and Telegraph Company; announcer Gayne Whitman, long associated with "The Telephone Hour"; the NBC engineer and yours truly. Via earphones and loudspeaker we listened to the music coming from three thousand miles away until we heard the cut-in cue given by Floyd Mack, the New York announcer:

"The next voice you hear will be that of Gayne Whitman, coming to you from San Francisco's Telegraph Hill over the new microwave radio relay."

The Coit Memorial Tower, atop San Francisco's Telegraph Hill, was the west-coast origination point for the first transcontinental microwave transmission used in a commercial broadcast. From the tower, the sound waves were transmitted to a telephone building in Oakland, which lies beyond the horizon shown in this photograph.

Immediately, with no change in transmission quality, Whitman's voice was heard. Because it so well describes the route of the microwave's path across the nation, and because it carries with it much of the excitement of the occasion, herewith is an excerpt from the announcement read by him:

In the old days, a semaphore stood here on Telegraph Hill. Whenever a ship approached San Francisco Bay, the semaphore was used to relay the news of its arrival to the city below. Tonight on Telegraph Hill, the sound waves of my voice become electrical waves in the microphone before me. At a telephone building across the bay near Oakland, they are translated again into extremely short radio waves—micro-waves. From a tower atop the building, they are beamed thirty-three miles to a second tower where they are caught, amplified, and sent speeding on their way.

From tower to tower, my words are hurled—up over the high Sierras at an altitude of more than ten thousand feet, down across a corner of the Great Salt Lake, northward over Wyoming to cross the Continental Divide, then southeast again past old Fort Laramie toward Denver. Then the words start to plunge down the old Pioneer Trail along the South Platte River, over the broad prairies of Omaha. They fly across the rich plains of Iowa, leap the Mississippi and hurry on to Chicago. They flash past the great industrial cities—Gary, Toledo, Cleveland, Pittsburgh—over the Appalachian Mountains, from relay to relay until, from the 107th tower in the chain, the words are snatched from the air in New York to become part of 'The Telephone Hour.' And all this takes place in the tiniest fraction of a second.

"The Telephone Hour" was, of course, radio. But the ship had been christened and was sliding down the ways into the sea of network television. And the inaugural use of microwave as a means of transmission for nationwide television was even more auspicious than the use we had made of it in calling it to the nation's attention via radio. On September 4, 1951, President Harry Truman was seen and heard coast-to-coast as he addressed the Japanese Peace Treaty Conference in San Francisco.

Less than a month later, the first entertainment program to be carried across the nation by microwave appeared on the home screens: the "All-Star Theater" was broadcast on September 28th. The second coast-to-coast commercial TV program, "The Colgate Comedy Hour," was transmitted the very next day. It was a case of "The King is dead; long live the King!," for radio would step down as the great form of home entertainment. It would gradually assume a new form with the accent on news, disk jockeys, sports, talk shows, and more time given to the voices of minorities and special causes. Fred Allen, Henry Aldrich, "We the People," "Major Bowes's Original Amateur Hour," "Fibber McGee and Molly," "Amos 'n' Andy," and soap operas would give way to TV's Milton Berle, "Leave it to Beaver,"

"What's My Line?," Ed Sullivan, Lucille Ball, "Sanford and Son," and soap operas.

Among the few dramatic shows heard on radio today, "Heart-beat Theater" has probably had the longest run. The recorded, half hour inspirational series, produced for The Salvation Army, has been broadcast once a week for some 22 years; a total of well over 1,100 programs. Directed for the past several years by Don Hills, the program is still heard (at this writing) over about 400 stations in the United States.

Subsequent to the advent of network television, there have been sporadic revivals of comedy shows, serious dramatic shows and mystery shows. Even as this is being written, the CBS network clings tenaciously to its "Radio Mystery Theater." As recently as 1974, this author scripted 23 programs for "Rod Serling's Zero Hour," broadcast over the radio network of the

Baseball tycoon and former Western star of radio, Gene Autry, sings into an old-fashioned carbon mike with (l. to r.) comedian Ken Murray, announcer Harry Von Zell, and ventriloquist/comedian Edgar Bergen. The occasion was the celebration of the opening of the new Pacific Pioneer Broadcasters headquarters at the corner of Sunset Boulevard and Vine Street in Hollywood.

Norman Corwin: broadcasting pioneer. An innovator, creator of true radio "literature," and a skilled director and producer, Corwin was one of the real giants of the medium.

Mutual Broadcasting System, and—having come full cycle after 36 years—recently contributed adaptations of several Conan Doyle perennials to the "Sherlock Holmes Radio Theater," a projected syndication series starring Edward Mulhare as Holmes and Ben Wright as Dr. Watson.

But the former concept of radio programming merely glows feebly like embers in a dying fire—and the embers are not likely to be fanned into flames. However, as Norman Corwin, one of radio's most prolific and literate writers told a recent meeting of the Pacific Pioneer Broadcasters:

"If Muhammad Ali and button down collars can each make a comeback, so can an art that is younger than I am. And I don't feel old at all."

Well, regardless of how the younger broadcasters of today may refer to me, I certainly don't think of myself as an 'old fart'. So, if radio should rise again, wake me up. It's not that I'm tired; it's just that I fall asleep during the late late show.

Index

165